Estacada SAGAS

Kathryn Hurd

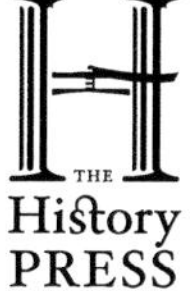

Published by The History Press
Charleston, SC
www.historypress.net

Front cover, top: *Fishing the Clackamas*, ©1994 Jenny Joyce and The Artback, renovated ©2011. Courtesy of The Artback; *bottom*: courtesy of Nancy Tedrow.
Back cover: courtesy of Nancy Tedrow; *insert*: *Welcome*, statue carved by Bobby Lehnen. Sign made for City of Estacada. *Courtesy of Mike Dille.*

Opposite: Estacada circa 1930s. Interactive map and history timeline available online at www.EstacadaHistory.com. *Historic Map by Jordan Winthrop & MapCloud.us.*

First published 2017

Manufactured in the United States

ISBN 9781467119672

Library of Congress Control Number: 2017934934

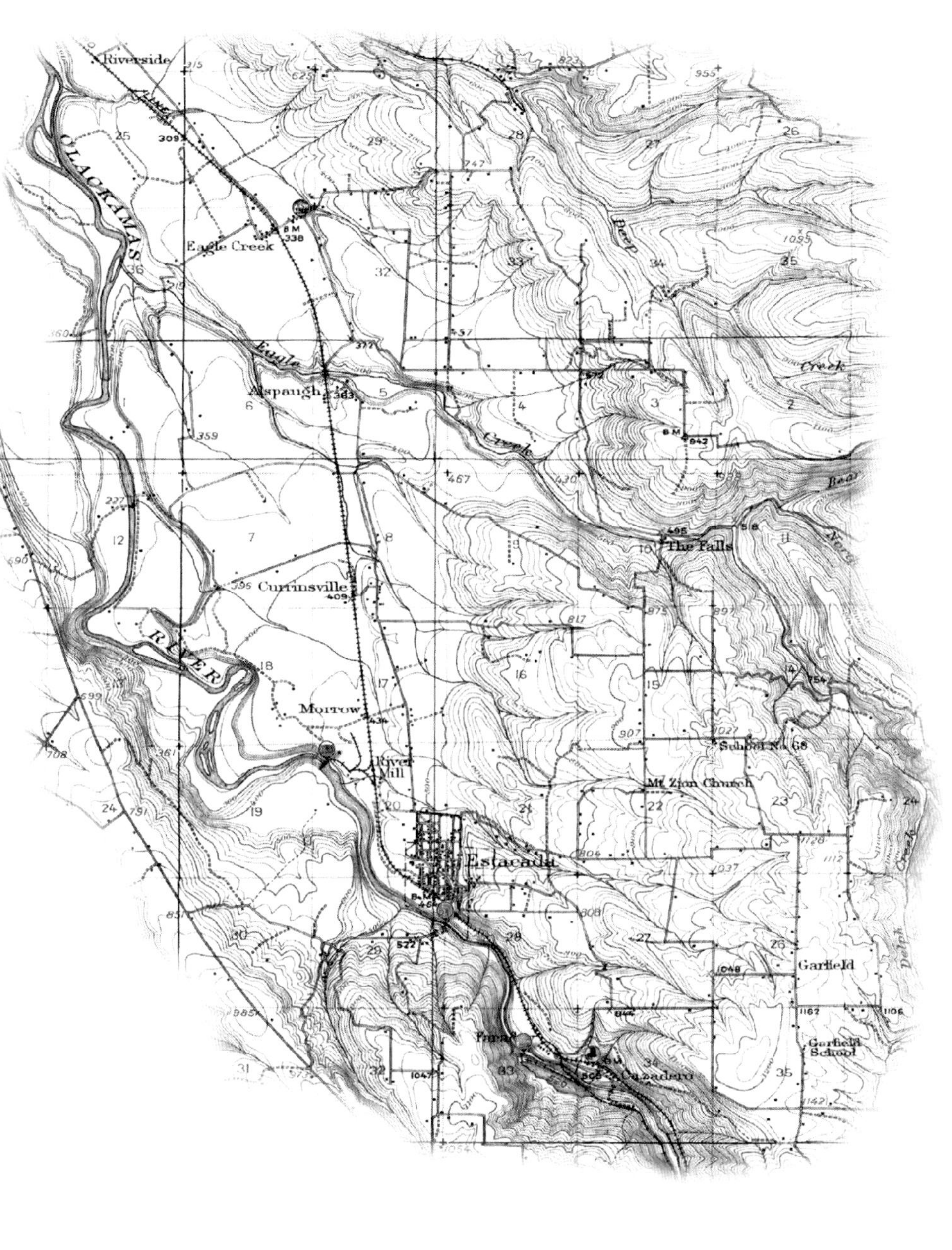

Riverside
CLACKAMAS
Eagle Creek
Eagle
Creek
Aspaugh
Currinsville
RIVER
Morrow
River Mill
Estacada
The Falls
School No 68
Mt Zion Church
Garfield
Garfield School
Cazadero

Contents

Foreword

In many American small towns, public libraries are the keepers of local history and culture. That is true in Estacada, current population 3,064, where our library keeps a print collection chronicling Estacada's past as well as historical information about its surrounding communities. Our collection includes the usual microfilmed newspapers, school yearbooks and maps. But if you want to read about Estacada's role in the only state-sponsored rock music festival in American history, we've got the book. Interested in our city's many original murals? Use our mural walk guide. Looking for an ancestor's headstone? Check the local pioneer cemetery inventories. Are you a quilter? You'll enjoy the photographic memoir about the handcrafting of the city of Estacada's centennial quilt by the Skip-a-Week Club, active since 1921. Our library has its own historic quilt, "The Community Book Shelf," also crafted by the Skip-a-Week Club, commemorating the new library in 2006. Local citizens donated funds to have quilt pieces embroidered with family names, words or phrases relevant to them. It hangs in our lobby, where its handiwork can be admired and the names it bears can be remembered.

Our collection is unique to Estacada and tells the story of a culture, time and place. If you look at the library's local history section (in the 979s, by the way), you'll notice that much of what we own was compiled by local people who wanted to tell the story of this town as they experienced it. The hand-typed remembrances and first-person accounts gleaned from newspapers and oral histories came from people in the early to mid-twentieth century and represent much of the historical information we have about this area. As time marches on, it becomes increasingly important to chronicle the stories told by our people before it's too late. Without these sagas, the gift of their observations is lost.

In *Estacada Sagas*, Kathryn Hurd adds to our oral history record, continuing from her first pictorial history collection, *Images of America: Estacada*. Her extensive research and outreach to find people willing to share their stories is again apparent.

I realized Kathryn's dedication to telling stories when she participated in the library's centennial celebration in 2013.

She performed a monologue as one of the "Library Ladies" who helped to found the library in 1913. She researched the library's own history archive to get all the details right and told our story with humor and affection. She was the hit of the program.

Estacada is richer for Kathryn's work and for how it informs our understanding of the city. We and our future citizens are grateful that she has given us these *Sagas*.

Michele D. Kinnamon, director
Estacada Public Library
January 2017

Acknowledgements

I am overwhelmed by the generosity of the people who made this book possible. Some told me a story about their family and shared accompanying personal photos. Others donated hours of their time in order to bring this book into being.

Thank you to the following people: Jack Reynolds, Audrey Wilson, Marilyn O'Grady, Leroy W. Layton, Jane Reid, Gary Warkentin, Tom Wille, Dorothy Sahr, Gloria Polzin, Teri Poppino, Bruce Poppino, Mike Whitten, Connie Redmond, Melanie Wagner, William B. Eliott, David Bugni, Jan Patterson, Jean McCloskey, Herm Saunders, John Poppino, Anna Marumm, Glen Wolcott, Emily Lindstrand, Kate Scrivener, Rose Wrangler Geraldine Morse, Phyllis Wahlstrom, Miriam Glover, Carl Prokop, Warren Barr, Bill Klaetsch, Bob Akins, Bob Brown, Dan Swanson, Dottie Genereaux, John Rhodes, Fred and Leona Campanella, Nancy Tedrow, Susie Rudisil, Janice Cheatham, Ray Horn, Chad Wheeler, Sarah Hibbert, Clackamas River Ranger District timber sale administrator Floyd Walker and, finally, at Estacada Les Schwab Tire Store, Kole Pearson; Terry White, manager; and Scott Schmid, assistant manager.

I am indebted to Alice Neely, Barb Hicks, Mike Misley, Mike Doolittle, Phil Lingelbach, Sylvia Bowman, Gilbert Shibley, Ruth Lazott and Wilma Guttridge, who fed me information and fielded a host of questions during my research; Michele Kinneman, who opened all the library resources for my use; Leslie Pearson and Jordan Winthrop, who provided technical assistance; Katinka Bryk, who responded quickly to any request and referred me to the resources I needed; Robert Steele, who provided technical hydroelectric dam language and statistics; Mary Ann Bugni, who created a communication database; and Mike Dille, who took beautiful photographs.

Andrea Anderson and Nolene Triska assisted me by reading and rereading stories and offering helpful suggestions. Pam Peterson supported me throughout the entire project, and I could not have completed the book without her. I give my deepest appreciation to Laura Whittemore, a copy editor who seems to understand everything.

I am most grateful to my wonderful editors, Ben Gibson and Rick Delaney, who proved to be encouraging, patient and supportive while providing the perfect answers to my questions.

Introduction

Books record and explore history. People change and make history. This is a book about people. Some are famous, others were known only by a few of their fellow residents, but all were unique.

Estacada has a rich and colorful history, and my goal in writing this book was to record some of that information before it is lost. Little of the history of this area was recorded and saved, so the primary source of information is in the hands and memories of those whose families have lived it.

I felt great pleasure in collecting the stories and images for this book. Each story was enlightening and fascinating; interestingly, many stories intertwined. Were it not for the recollections of these wonderful people, this history would be lost forever.

I recorded everything as people related their stories and left the names as they were at the time of the story, although some have since changed. Squaw Mountain, named before Estacada was founded, is now Tumala Mountain, and the names of other roads have been changed, as well. The local newspaper has been known as *Estacada News* but also *Clackamas County News* and the *Progress*.

Over three thousand people live within the city limits, but more than eighteen thousand people who also call Estacada home live in the surrounding unincorporated communities of Garfield, Springwater, Dodge, Viola, Currinsville, George, Eagle Creek and Porter. The residents share a long history—settlers began arriving to the area as early as 1850.

If, after reading this book, you would like to learn more about us, visit the Estacada Public Library and view the interactive map and history timeline available online at www.EstacadaHistory.com.

Inside this book are historic stories from the mouths of the people who lived them. Enjoy.

1
Big Beginnings

What's In a Name?

Few topics create more interest among local residents than how Estacada got its name.

In the mid-1800s, the Clackamas River territory attracted hundreds of people searching for a new life in the West. These were tough, independent, hardworking individuals. Some may have also been hard drinking, because the community was originally known as Whiskey Flats.

The first bridge across the Clackamas River near the settlement was created in 1859 from trees felled across the river. It broke down completely when a herd of cattle was driven across it in 1862. Tragically, the bovines perished in the fall or by drowning. The fallen timbers were replaced by a wooden structure, built above the water's current, allowing settlers heading to California gold fields access to a road that passed through Springwater and Viola, an easier route than the one through Oregon City. Travelers went to the little town now called High Bridge.

The origins of the first two names are fairly straightforward, but a century-long controversy surrounds the source of the permanent moniker. There are several theories, all of which are the result of the Morris Brothers Investment Bankers headquartered in Portland, Oregon.

By 1901, the city of Portland, hungry for electric power, grew increasingly reliant on an extensive electrified network of trolleys for transportation.

Introduction of electric lights and newly unveiled electric appliances increased the need for power.

Morris Brothers formed the Oregon Water & Power Company (OW&P) and directed George W. Brown, its chief engineer, to search out a location for a new hydroelectric plant. The Clackamas River appeared to have possibilities, so Brown hired John Zobrist to guide him up the river. They found the ideal spot a short distance above High Bridge.

In 1903, the Morris Brothers Investment Bankers formed Oregon Water Power & Railway (OWP&R). The firm laid rails up the Clackamas River to move supplies and manpower for the building of Cazadero Dam and Faraday Powerhouse.

Then Morris Brothers formed the Oregon Water & Power Township Company and bought all the land from the Zobrist, Pierce and Williams claims. The purpose of the township company was to capitalize on the railroad by selling land and creating a town below the dam. An advertising campaign used the railroad to draw potential landowners up the river and encourage city dwellers to take a relaxing round-trip to a scenic paradise. The company built a grand hotel and a beautiful park along the river as enticements.

On December 27, 1903, OW&P Township Company president C.W. Morrow, land agent W.P. Keady, his assistant George W. Kelly and

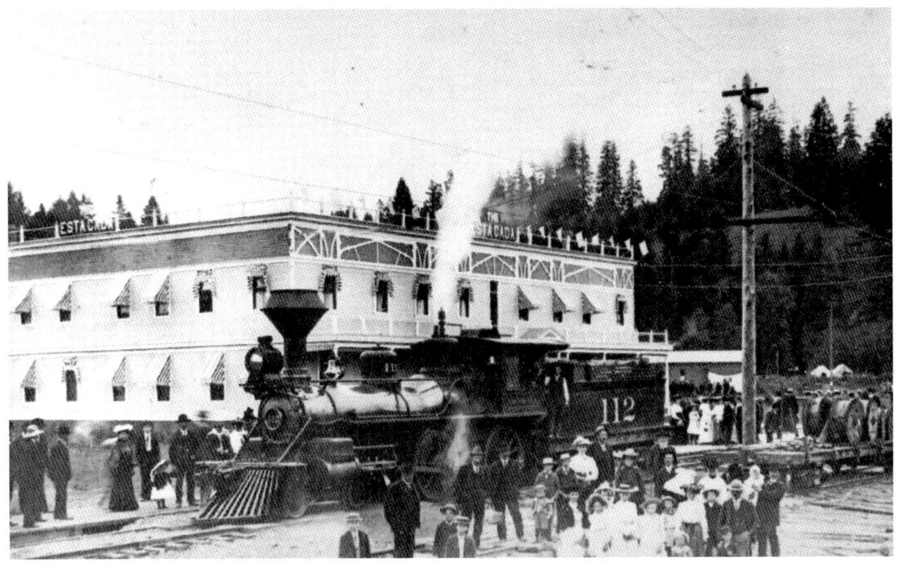

Travelers taking the train disembarked beside the Estacada Hotel, which was the town's prestigious landmark hostelry and restaurant from 1903 to 1929. *Courtesy of Nancy Tedrow.*

OWP&R president and railway manager W.H. Hurlburt met in the township company office at First and Alder Streets in downtown Portland to choose a name for the new town. Each man placed a slip of paper with a proposed name in a hat. The name on the paper that was drawn was Estacada. Or was it? And what does the name mean? A few theories propose the answer.

Claim no. 1: George P. Kelly saw the name *Estacado* on a map of the United States and liked the sound of it. In western Texas and eastern New Mexico, the term *llano Estacado* means "staked plan" in Spanish. Thinking that Estacada sounded more "American," he changed the last letter before putting it in the hat.

Claim no. 2: George Kelly suggested Estacado, but the sign maker misinterpreted the name. Thinking it was a misspelling, he penned the last letter as an "a." Perhaps Estacada got its name from an early twentieth-century version of a typo.

Claim no. 3: Estacada is a combination of Esther Williams, from whom Morris Brothers had purchased much of the land on which the town was built, and Morrow's land agent, Mr. Keady. The name *Keady* was pronounced "Cady." Hence, *Esther* plus *Cady* equals *Estacada.*

Nearly a dozen emotional handwritten documents have been signed attesting to the "correct" source and meaning of the name. The only point on which they agree is that the name was drawn from a hat. Now, over a century later, speculation still exists. "How did Estacada get its name?" The question remains unanswered.

ESTACADA HOTEL

The hotel was resplendent with natural woods. Furniture of precious woods, wicker and bamboo graced its forty-seven rooms. Once construction was completed in 1903, advertising material published by Oregon Power & Railway Company touted the hotel as "a modest, homelike, and comfortable inn, where the visitor may make his home and headquarters during his vacation."

The following quote appeared in the menu of the Portland Restaurant, inside the Estacada Hotel:

He may live without books.
What is knowledge but grieving?

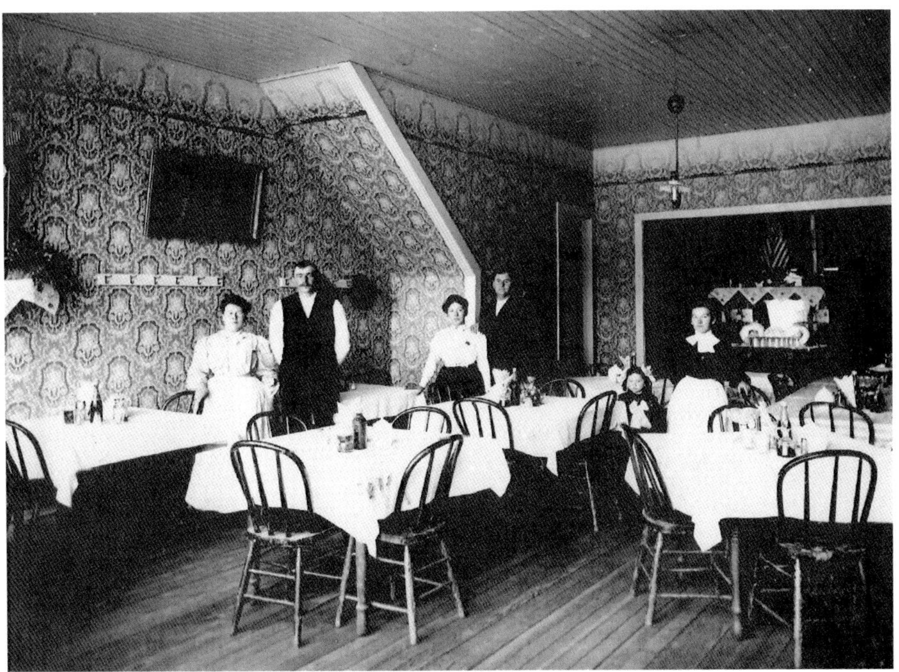

Inside the hotel. The family-run Portland Restaurant dining room was popular with visitors and townspeople alike. *Courtesy of Nancy Tedrow.*

He may live without hope.
What is hope but decaying?
He may live without love
What is passion but pining?
But where is the man who can live without dining?

ESTACADA PARK

Originally, the railroad transported workers and equipment to build Cazadero Dam, but Oregon Water Power & Railway increased its investment by designing the park to entice Portlanders to make a two-and-one-half-hour trolley trip to Estacada. At one time, it took five trolleys a day to carry all the visitors to the city. The largest group was the Portland Employees Organization picnic in 1922, when attendees came by a four-car electric train for baseball games, sack races, music, dancing and strolling through the park.

The sixty-acre park extended west from the covered bridge over the Clackamas River all the way to the site of River Mill Dam. A path traversed the entire length, providing a view of the Clackamas River rapids for those who came for excursions or parties. A stairway led down the bank to a platform at water level, where anglers were rewarded with a plentiful catch of trout.

Visitors and local families posed for photographs under the lovely arched entrance to Estacada Park. Welcoming visitors for the first time in October 1906, the park proved to be a valuable attraction until 1922. Not far from the park entrance was a gazebo, a graceful structure that was built for local musicians to entertain picnickers with a summer concert. It was also a romantic setting for lovers. A pavilion adjacent to the gazebo housed a piano and "masks for dancing parties."

As automobile travel increased and interest in the railway waned, Oregon Water Power & Railway sold the park land to the Portland Telegram Subscription Department. In turn, for thirty-five dollars, Portland Telegram sold a two-year subscription to the newspaper plus title to a small twenty-foot by one-hundred-foot lot for a summer cabin.

Hello, Are You There?

In 1905, barely thirty years after Alexander Graham Bell invented the telephone, the Estacada telephone office was erected by M.C. Adkins. This was a cooperative venture among Adkins, B.O. Brownwell, John B. Hairant, J.W. Reed and R.A. Stralter.

In the beginning, residents of Estacada desiring a telephone bought a share of stock in the cooperative. Membership was limited (if twenty members on one party line can be called limited). A stock share included installation of the oblong oak wood crank telephone on the wall in the kitchen.

For people living on a farm in an outlying area, acquiring phone service was a bit more complicated. Granville Linn, for example, had to buy his own phone, probably from Montgomery Ward. He had to buy the batteries, wire, connectors, insulators and poles. On top of that, he had to install his own phone and run his line from the farmhouse to the main Currinsville telephone line.

Conversations were carried on two bare wires, the kind used to train berries, wrapped together. In Estacada, telephone poles were installed.

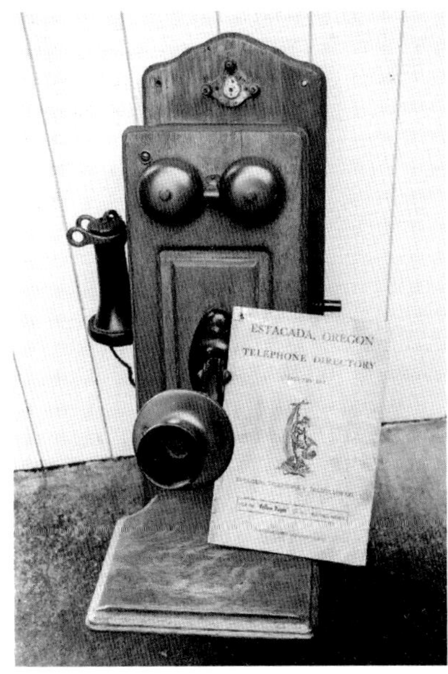

A phone like this one hung on the kitchen wall in most Estacada-area homes from the 1880s to the 1920s. *Courtesy of Mike Doolittle.*

Out in the country, however, the wires were attached to trees and makeshift suspension holders and, in a few cases, run along the barbed wire on top of a fence. Wind and rain interfered with the uninsulated wires, in many cases causing conversations to cut out. We can sympathize with those callers, since losing contact while on the phone can be frustrating even with today's technology.

The phone box in the kitchen was placed at about head height so that it would be easy to speak into the mouthpiece by standing in front of it. The receiver, attached by a cord, was cradled on a hook on the left side of the telephone box. The telephone book was suspended on a string from a hook or nail beside the phone.

If a person wanted to talk to someone, she removed the receiver and turned the crank on the right-hand side of the box, which alerted the operator at the switchboard in the phone company office. Operators could connect a customer to another house or business or switch to long-distance assistance in Portland. If the operator wasn't busy, she would sometimes chat a bit before ringing the number desired.

When a call came into a home, it jangled the pair of bells on the top part of the front of the phone. Each home was assigned a "code" ring, such as two short rings and one long ring, or one short and one long, to alert the family that a call was coming in. Early on in Springwater, a person removed the receiver and turned the crank in the code ring to call another family on the party line without going through a main switchboard.

Neighbors soon learned who was being called by the code of rings. Calls were supposed to be private, although listening in on a neighbor's calls (called "rubbering on the line") was a common practice, ostensibly out of concern. In times of illness, neighbors seldom phoned the home, depending instead on the neighborhood listening service for information.

If someone wanted to know what was going on at a particular home, all that was necessary was to listen for the ring and quietly slip the receiver off the hook. This was such a common practice that a third party (listener) often joined in the conversation, making it three-way or, at times, four-way. Such a situation was not much different than the modern-day coffee break.

What an evolution! Telephone communication has advanced further than Alexander Graham Bell could have imagined. From turning a crank with a code ring, to alerting an operator to connect you, to dialing a landline, to pushing buttons on a cellphone. Bell would probably call it magic—and so it is.

Read All About It

In 1913, Estacada was a thriving town. Every day, five trolleys arrived from Portland carrying city dwellers who wanted to enjoy a picnic and stroll along the river in the serene countryside. The OWPCO had built a pavilion at Estacada Park to provide a place for dances and other gatherings. On nice weekends, in addition to regular enclosed cars, the trolleys had as many as five open cars—aptly named pneumonia cars—on each run.

River Mill Dam was a couple of years old. Many buildings had electric lights, but the streets were dark after sundown. The city's core was divided into small lots so that businesses would be centrally located. Many store owners lived above their shops, although some private residences were mixed in.

A stroll through downtown was an adventure in sights and sounds. Grocery stores sold bags and barrels of sugar, coffee, beans and other food residents couldn't raise. The front counter displayed mapleine and a variety of candy treats. On handy shelves behind the counter stood bottles of castor oil, used to reverse the effects of the candy. Palace Meat Market carried fresh beef, pork, poultry and lamb.

Women bought fabrics and sewing materials at Reed and Hall Dry Goods and patronized Dale's Millinery for their stunning hats. Friends met for lunch at the grand Estacada Hotel or at Marchbank's Café, famous for its scrumptious fresh raspberry pie.

Next door to Marchbank's, the Family Theater showed motion pictures on Saturday and Sunday nights. In 1913, it advertised a stage production called *A Good Minstrel*.

Near Ed Bohnert's photography studio on Broadway, Doctor Haviland lived above the combination drugstore and post office run by his brother

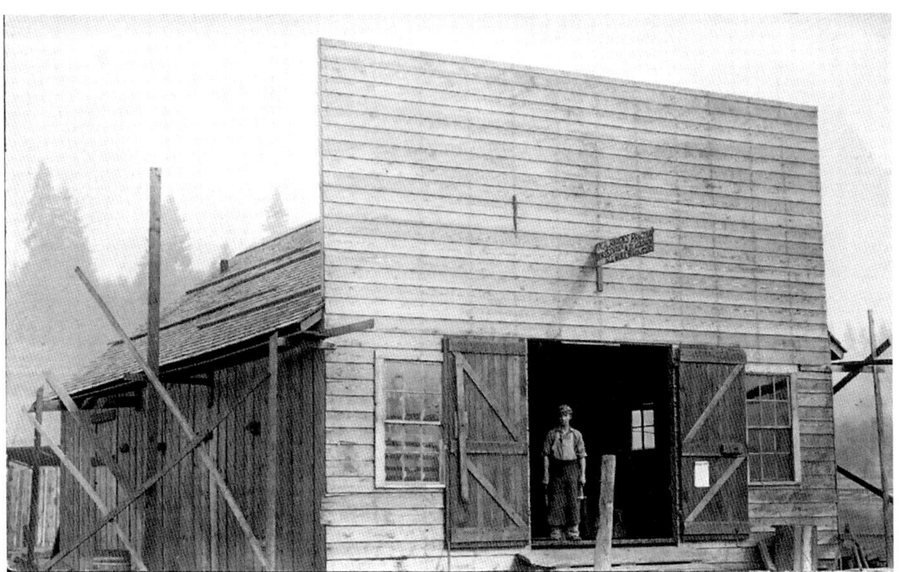

In 1920, the William A. Rhodes blacksmith shop provided service on the upper level of Estacada. *Courtesy of John Rhodes.*

John. Mr. McCurdy and Mr. Cary ran the two hardware stores that supplied hardworking farmers with shovels, rakes, hoes and plows. Dubois Lumber was nearby on Main Street. Mr. Barr and Mr. Carpenter, the two town blacksmiths, shoed horses and created metalwork.

Outside the main business district was a brick-making plant with its distinctive smoke stack, a cannery and the Garfield cheese factory. Dairy herds were a familiar sight, but the town became excited when a dead cow was found in the water supplying the Estacada Reservoir. The city passed an ordinance prohibiting the running at large or herding of any horse, cattle or mule on any streets or alleys of the city between the hours of 7:00 in the evening and 6:00 in the morning. Young people could stay out until their 9:00 p.m. curfew

Games played by the city's new baseball and football clubs were well-attended events. A rod-and-gun club and even a tennis club provided camaraderie. The Currinsville Band held concerts and played songs prior to local theatrical productions, such as the Garfield Grange's performance of the comic play *Thompson's Hired Man*.

Those wanting spiritual sustenance could find it at their desired congregation: Methodist, Baptist, Presbyterian or Catholic. On the other hand, men gathered at the billiard parlor or had a stiff drink at the Blind Pig

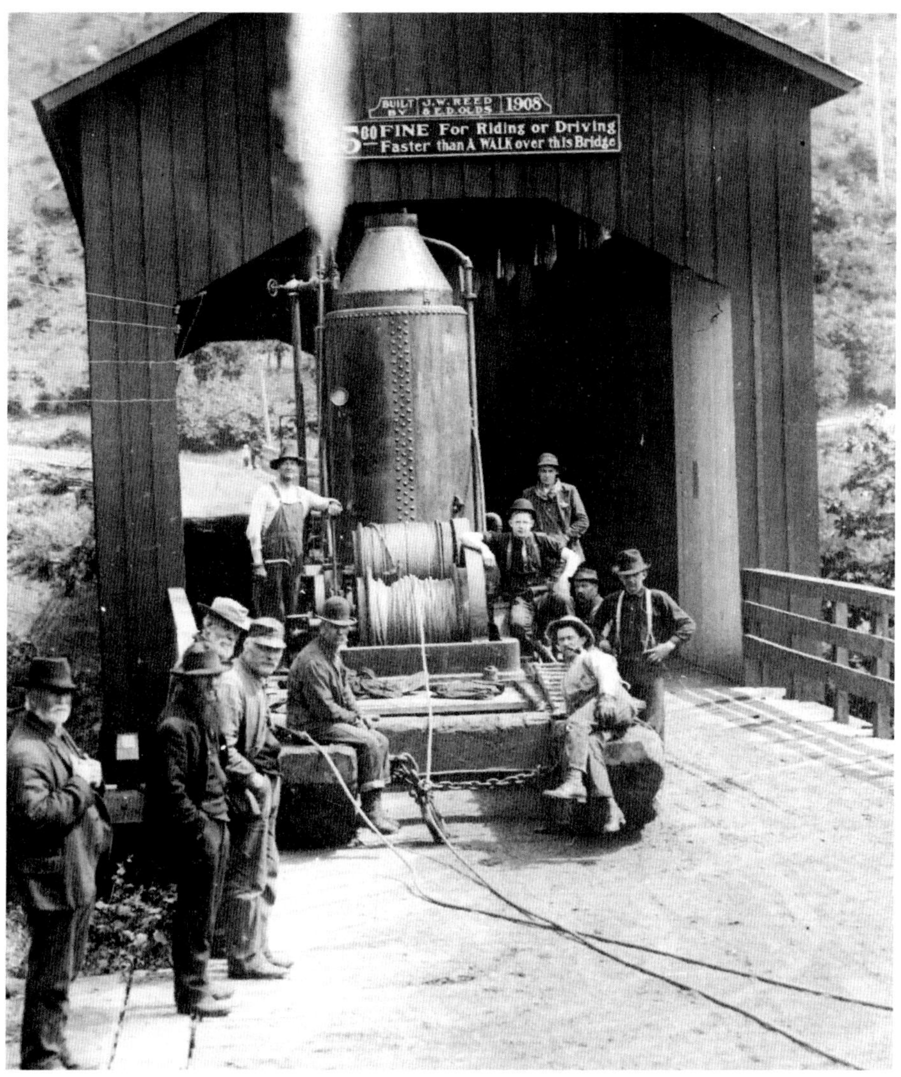

J.W. Reed engineered construction of the third bridge crossing from Estacada to the Springwater side of the Clackamas River. *Courtesy of Jackknife-Zion-Horseheaven Historical Society.*

Saloon and Brothel or at a plethora of other saloons. Some maintained that there were more saloons than churches, but this was an exaggeration. They were actually even in number.

After eight years, J.W. Reed, real estate agent, contractor and builder of the famous covered bridge across the Clackamas River, announced he was finally stepping down as the city's mayor.

Into this diverse mix of activities, twenty-eight ladies gathered to form the Civic Improvement Club (CIC), an organization that brought culture and civility to Estacada. The women formed committees to raise funds by way of Halloween, Thanksgiving and Valentine's Day dances at the Estacada Park Pavilion. They sponsored concerts, held rummage sales and gave a Martha Washington Tea. The first project paid for by these funds was the installation of lights and the placement of benches on the main streets.

The club sponsored the city's first "Cleaning Up Day," an event in recognition of the fact that there was no city dumping ground. CIC then led the city to find a common dumping site, working toward securing land for a children's playground. The greatest achievement of the Civic Improvement Club was the beginning of the Estacada Library.

Hattie Saunders moved from Canada with her husband and children. Hattie had agreed to move on the condition that the new town had a school, a Methodist church and a library. She found two of the three in Estacada. Hattie immediately became a member of the Civic Improvement Club. At her urging, in 1913, the women formed a committee to create a sort of lending library, news of which was duly reported in the local newspaper, the *Progress*.

The CIC committee convinced Mary Adams, owner of the Estacada Mercantile, to rent them some space in her store. The women brought books from their own collections to the store to lend to avid readers. Each woman knew all the books they owned and remembered who borrowed which book.

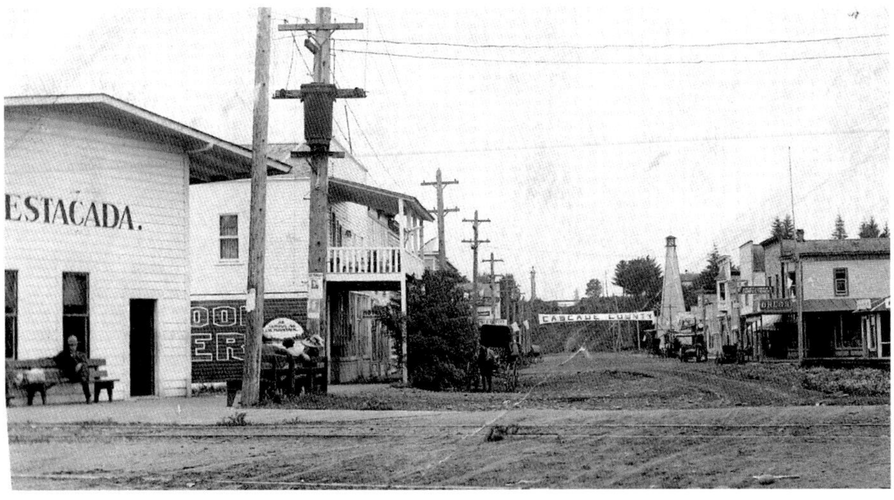

Looking north on Broadway Street in 1930. *Courtesy of Alice Neely.*

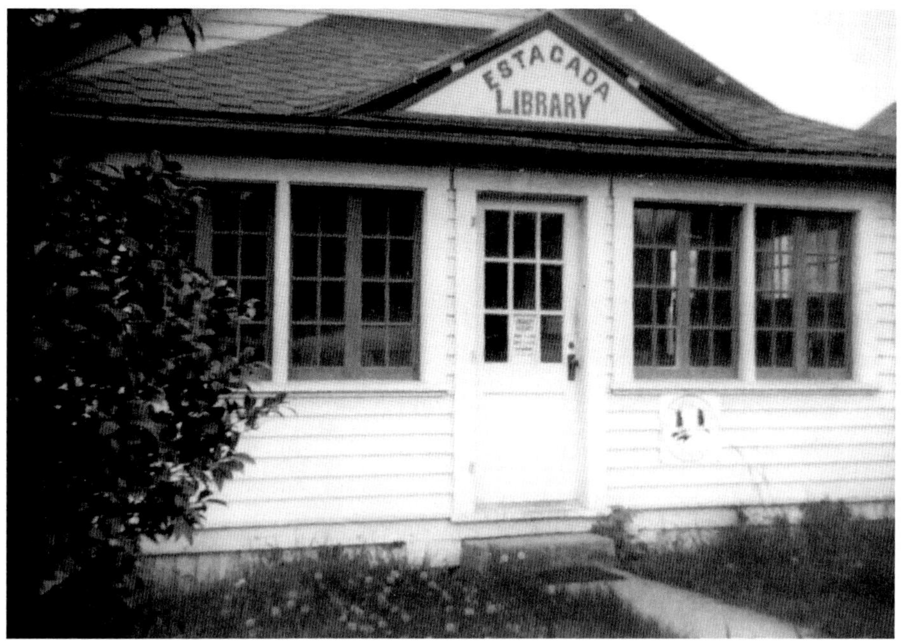

The little cottage on Broadway belonging to Mrs. Nina Eckar became the first library for the town of Estacada. *Courtesy of Barb Hicks.*

As the number of readers grew, the CIC committee needed more space. On May 13, 1919, the Civic Improvement Club became the Estacada Library Association. In September 1922, the Estacada Library Association became incorporated.

The International Order of Odd Fellows hall stood on the corner of Third and Broadway. This was the tallest building in town, towering over the other businesses on the street. Across the street to the west stood a cottage belonging to Nina Eckar. Beginning in 1920, she generously allowed the CIC women to use the sun porch of her house as a reading room for children, and she allowed her parlor and its shelves to serve as the main library. Over the door, the ladies painted the words "Public Library Reading Room." Eckar was librarian from 1921 to 1937.

The association voted to buy the cottage. It took months of planning and hard work. The women held dozens of fundraisers and finally had enough money to purchase Mrs. Eckar's house as a permanent site for the library. The mortgage was paid off on July 1, 1923.

In the article "Library Day This Saturday," the *Progress* invited readers to contribute to the new library: "Everyone is urged to bring as many books as you can spare. A public library is to be established in Estacada. The books that are donated will only be starters in the enterprise." The following week, the *Progress* reported that citizens had contributed eighty-eight books and the Methodist church nearly one hundred more. The sign above the door of Eckar's cottage now read, "Estacada Library."

Although many women contributed, Hattie Saunders's strong resolve and tireless effort earned her a reputation as first official "Library Lady."

Patrons walked up a short sidewalk through the gate in the picket fence to the small porch and the front door. The check-out desk was on the left, inside the front door. Each room in the cottage was a section of the library: fiction, nonfiction, children's literature, periodicals and so on. Catalogue cards, arranged in the Dewey Decimal System, were used to find books, but the volunteer Library Ladies were happy to help patrons locate a volume of their choice.

Patrons paid one dollar a year and five cents for each book checked out. Up to three books at a time could be kept for two weeks. To check out a book, a patron wrote his or her name on a card kept in a pocket glued inside the back cover and left it with the Library Lady of the day. Cards were kept in a file box on the desk.

As time went on, the Library Ladies aged, and some passed away. The surviving members informed the city that they wished to stop operating the library and offered to donate their facilities to the city. On March 3, 1960, the city passed an ordinance establishing the free Estacada Public Library. Sometime later, the books were moved to the Estacada City Hall building on Main Street.

The little cottage that had housed the library for so many years was sold and moved to the upper level on Zobrist Street. The sun porch was removed, and the cottage lives on again as a family residence.

The library took over the 2,800-square-foot south wing of the 1930s city hall with its sunny windows and handsome fireplace. Library services and activities unite a community, and this was definitely the case in Estacada. In addition to stocking the shelves and checking out volumes, new and creative Library Ladies began holding weekly storytelling sessions for children. Special events became common: a renaissance fair fundraiser, a summer reading program with prizes and a storytelling festival with professional readers thrilling the crowd.

The cozy space gradually filled with bookcases and shelves to accommodate the increasing number of volumes until patrons were nearly obliged to turn sideways to move in the aisles. Thousands of books lay tucked away in storage. The teen section was in a closet, the children's area was a cubby-sized corner. A restroom with one stall served everyone who visited.

In 2004, plans began to materialize for building a new, twelve-thousand-square-foot library. Estacada residents attended town hall meetings to give their input on what they wanted the library to look like. Making it a reality required the creation of a special taxing district that encompassed the existing Estacada School District boundaries, passing a $1.9 million bond and obtaining numerous grant awards. An anonymous donor gave $180,000 to help purchase the 0.77-acre building site. Volunteers of America donated Wade Creek Pond to the city. Another anonymous donor contributed $150,000 toward construction of a community room in the library.

The Estacada Library Foundation worked on fundraising. Local artist Nancy Cundill donated handcrafted jewelry for a fundraiser. Members of the community contributed what they could in an outpouring of funds and volunteer hours. Library director Beth McKinnon spent over one thousand volunteer hours ensuring the project's success.

In the summer of 2006, the library staff and volunteers began the task of moving. Patrons were asked to check out fifty items, take them home, keep them safe for up to two months and return them to the new library after it opened. Over several weeks, books were gradually returned, checked in and placed on the spacious shelves in their appropriate section. The staff breathed a sigh of relief, saying, "That was easy."

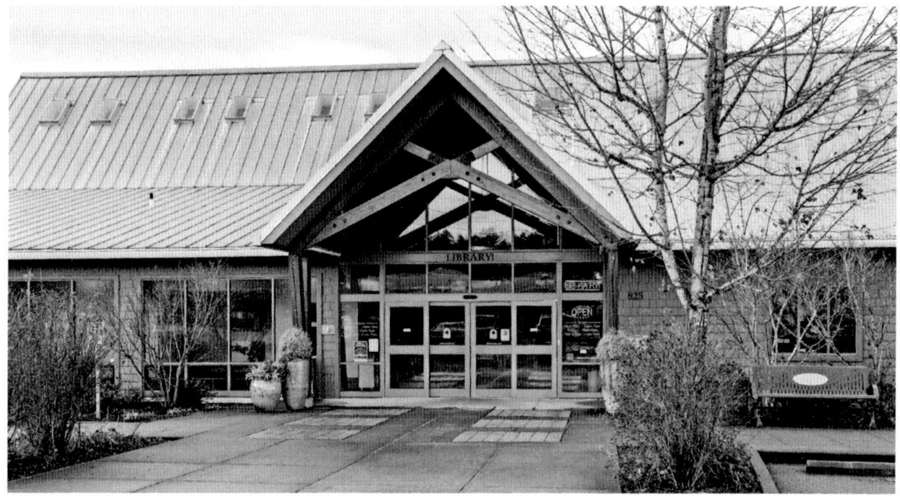

The front doors of the beautiful new library welcome patrons to browse through thousands of volumes. *Courtesy of Mike Dille.*

On August 6, 2006, the new Estacada Public Library opened its doors. Patrons were greeted by high wood-trussed ceilings and huge sun-lit windows facing Wade Creek Pond. In the center of the room, a majestic two-sided stone fireplace is surrounded by comfortable chairs. Tables hold thirty public computers, including five children's educational computers. Other tables along the sunny windows provide areas for study and writing.

Bookshelves extend outward on both sides of the central area. The ninety Douglas fir shelf ends were made by an all-volunteer crew out of locally donated materials. Art donated by local artists hangs from walls. The Flora Community Room occupies the south end of the building. Nearby are two spacious restrooms.

A library is truly the heart of a community. Construction of the new Estacada Public Library was the product of visionaries who recognized that a library, especially in a small town, represents hope for the future. Its existence is a monument to the tireless Library Ladies over nearly one hundred years who made it possible.

Lunchtime

Prior to 1946, there was no such thing as a school lunch program. Most students walked several miles to school, carrying a lunch bucket with food to eat at noon. A fried-egg sandwich would taste so good in the middle of a long school day.

In the early days, a lard bucket was the container used most often as a lunch box, since it was commonly available and had a handle that made it easy to carry. This worked really well, unless you grabbed the wrong bucket on your way out of the house and discovered you had only lard for lunch.

2

The Damed-est River in Oregon

Explosion at River Mill

It was after noon on Saturday, March 2, 1911, when Mrs. Fisher learned about the explosion. She had dinner ready for her boarders, with her biscuits in a pan, when she was summoned to her neighbor's house. Mr. Dodds met her at the door.

"Please take a chair," he said kindly. "I have something to tell you. Your son Bud was killed in an explosion of the donkey boiler at just after seven this morning."

Mrs. Fisher's mind reeled at the news. Only the previous Thursday, she, Bud and his son Roy had moved from Sellwood to the temporary frame-and-tent town near the dam site outside Estacada. The Fishers settled in a three-bedroom house amid a little grove of trees, cheered by flowers growing around the cozy homes of nearby neighbors.

The Fisher home had already attracted several boarders. Mrs. Fisher, although over seventy years old, was active and spry. Her grandson could stack wood, build a fire and help with the upkeep of the house. The income from the boarders would help pay the family's living expenses.

Bud Fisher, long the sole supporter of his widowed mother, would make three dollars a day as a member of the logging crew until the dam's scheduled completion in October. The crew of eight men pulled logs from the neighboring hillside toward River Mill by means of a donkey engine powered by a forty-horsepower steam boiler. The logs were milled for use in the framework holding the cement for the dam.

Mrs. Fisher's voice quavered as she asked Mr. Dodds, "How did it happen?"

"From what we know," said Dodds, "Thalmar Negvist, fireman of the donkey, built a fire under the boiler, checked the water level and returned to the boardinghouse one-half mile away. After he and the other members of the crew finished eating breakfast, they all gathered to warm their hands by the boiler before commencing work. The boiler blew up at 7:05, killing your son and five other men. Two were badly injured and are not expected to survive."

"Why did it explode?" she implored. Indeed, when such a tragedy occurs, we all ask "why?"

Dodds continued. "For several days, it is said, the safety valve on the boiler did not work properly. A number of experiments were carried out with improvised devices. Only this morning, William Pittman, one of the two brothers who contracted to get the logs to the mill, started for Portland with the express intention of purchasing a new valve. His brother James, who was acting as temporary engineer, was one of those killed."

Mrs. Fisher thought back to that morning. She had risen at five o'clock to fix breakfast for her son. Bud was ready to leave when young Roy, who often tagged along after his father, begged to go with him. Bud's reply rang in Mrs. Fisher's head: "No, you mustn't go. You might get killed."

She remembered hearing a blast. Roy wanted to know what it was, and she had said, "It's just more blasting for the dam." But it wasn't. It marked her son's death. Now Bud was gone, as were five other men.

What Mr. Dodds didn't want to describe to the grieving woman were the details of the horrific event. Ray Hamilton, a member of the crew, was late getting on the job that morning. He was between the sawmill and the donkey when the explosion occurred. He said the heavy boiler "floated through the air as if it were a man's hat driven by a gust of wind."

In fact, the boiler was thrown five hundred feet into the air, turning and twisting until it struck the ground a quarter of a mile away. The earth shook as it bored six feet down and tore up the soil for twenty feet around. The men were blown 5 to 150 feet away. The terrible loss of life and the gruesome sight of mutilated dead bodies in the thick underbrush of the swampy woodland made even the strongest men shrink from the scene.

Mrs. Fisher made a phone call to her daughter to relay the awful news. It was some time before her son-in-law Steve arrived to escort Mrs. Fisher back to Sellwood. During the trip, Steve attempted to calm the grief-stricken

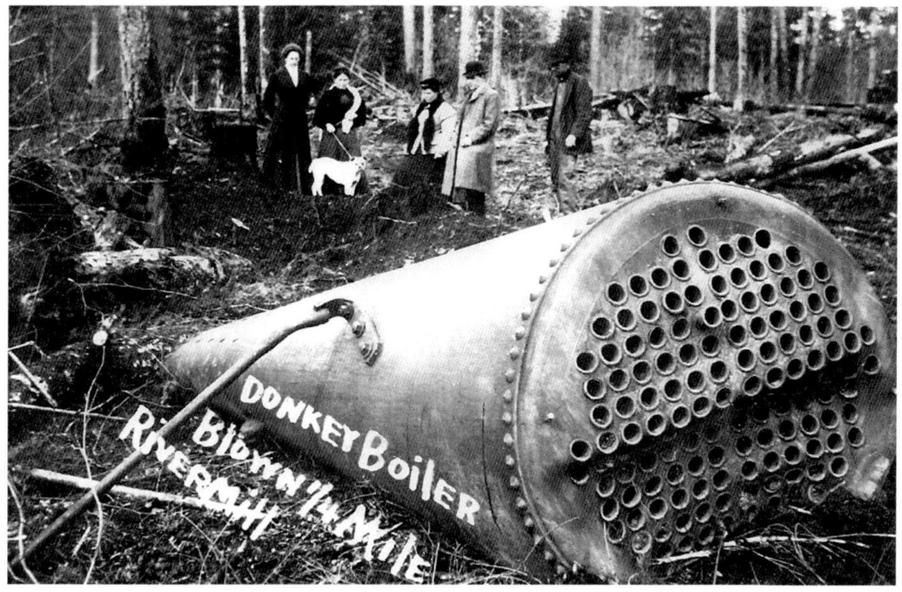

Once the bodies were removed, onlookers stood around in disbelief, surveying the ground littered with broken trees and mangled machinery. *Courtesy of Jack Reynolds.*

woman. He related that, only a week before, Bud had told him, "I'm going to live a different life." The following day, Sunday, Bud had asked Steve to go with him to attend a meeting especially for men.

Steve said, "When the preacher invited all who intended to live right to come and give him their hand, Bud was the first to get up and make the start. And his talk and actions after that proved to me that he was not lost. I want you to know that he had forgiven everybody, and that he did not hold aught against anyone on earth."

Roy spoke up. "If the good man has got my papa, let him have him. But what about us?"

Mrs. Fisher sighed, reached out and patted her grandson's hand. "A way will be provided."

Two of Mrs. Fisher's sons-in-law identified Bud's body at the undertaker's office in Portland. They were the only two to see Bud after he went to work that morning. Quite a crowd gathered for the funeral, and they expressed their sympathy for Mrs. Fisher and the families of the other men killed that day. Bud was buried in a nice casket that cost $125.

River Mill Dam was completed on schedule. At 11:00 a.m. on November 7, 1911, the gates of the dam were closed. Water backed up and formed a mild

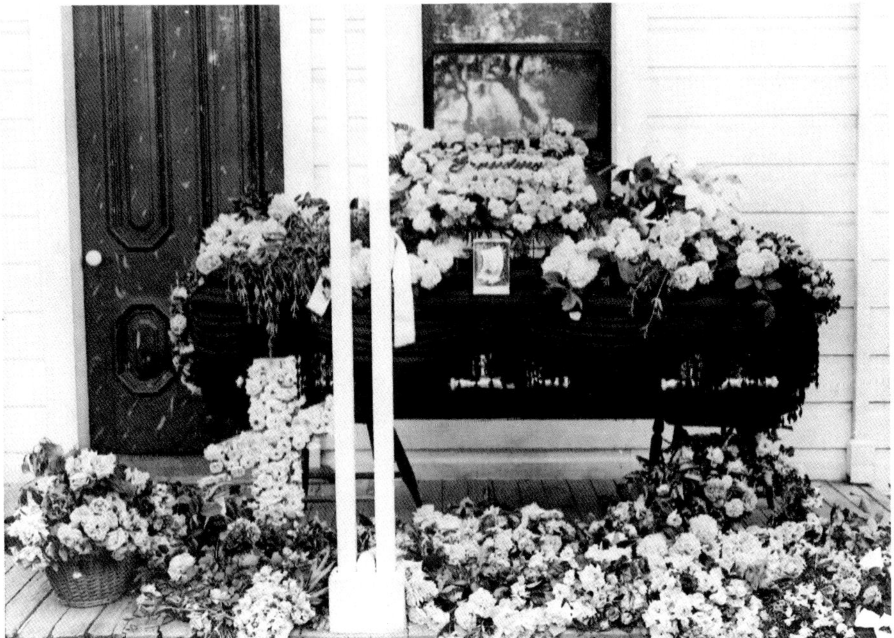

According to custom, Bud Fisher's casket stayed at the home for three days while family and friends paid their respects. *Courtesy of Jackknife-Zion-Horseheaven Historical Society.*

and placid stream where once had been turbulent and swift-flowing waters. The backwater, named Estacada Lake, rose eighty feet to come within twenty feet of the dam's spillway. Three of five penstocks, eleven feet in diameter, were opened. The penstocks delivered nine hundred cubic feet of water per second to each turbine. The turbines generated power that flowed through lines to run Portland trolleys, electric lights and many labor-saving devices.

Seven hundred men built the River Mill Dam. Four hundred were skilled. Three hundred were common laborers. Eight men were killed on March 2, 1911. They will be remembered.

THE TRESTLE

On Thursday, July 11, 1918, trainman H.D. "Harry" Kleinline leaned out the window as his Portland Railway, Light & Power Company (PRL&P) train crossed the 120-foot-tall wood trestle bridge over Estacada Lake. The trestle's timbers were reflected in the water below. The bridge was built before the construction of River Mill Dam. Rising water behind the completed dam had submerged the supporting timbers until the track sat only 35 feet above the lake.

Sunlight glinted on small ripples, and a slight breeze carried with it the faintest hint of oregano. The plant grew wild on the banks near the dam, seeded seven years earlier when the herb fell from Greek construction workers' lunches.

Conductor Arthur Kinder pointed to where the wide expanse of lake began to narrow. "That reminds me of my wife's favorite silk scarf, all blue and green with silver threads."

The locomotive could reach fifty miles an hour on open track, but engineer William Murray barely inched the train along the spur of the Cazedero Line to the south side of the Clackamas River.

Several months earlier, the bridge had been closed due to concerns about its condition. But inspectors had declared the bridge safe. Merchants in Estacada and Springwater waited anxiously for the train's arrival so they could again ship and receive goods shore-to-shore, a service only the train could provide. It was equipped with two electric engines, one at either end of the two freight cars. This allowed the crew to bring the train into Estacada and then return without turning the engine around.

On the other side of the bridge, William Murray brought the engine to the end of the line. He, Harry Kleinline and brakeman Thomas Kearney jumped down. William walked to the opposite end of the train and climbed into what was now the front engine. Harry and Thomas threw a series of switches to change the direction of the rails and couple and uncouple cars as the engine pulled back and forth. Now the two freight cars that had arrived with the train stood on the siding, and the new shipments sat between the two locomotives.

The final switch was turned, the tracks led straight ahead to the trestle and Thomas and Harry climbed back aboard. William called out, "Harry, I am fortunate to have a job I like so much."

Near noon, the engine pulled away from the station and began the return trip. The entire train had rolled out onto the trestle when Harry felt a trembling under his feet. In seconds, the trestle began to fall apart.

It happened so quickly that the crew had no time to react. With a terrible groan from the timbers and a mournful wail from the horn, the engines and freight cars slid down the tracks and plunged into the lake. In minutes the locomotives, cars and cargo had settled to the bottom eighty-five feet down. An eddy broke the surface, and then all was still.

Underwater, Harry struggled away from the sinking debris and rose, coughing and sputtering but unhurt, to the surface. "Help!" he called. But there was no need. The sickening sound of the collapse had brought people running. Locals picking blackberries on the shore gave an immediate alarm. Estacada firemen and PRL&P officials arrived. A crew from Faraday Dam sped to the scene.

Before help arrived, Harry heard a cry from Thomas, who was caught in the timbers. Harry made his way to his fellow crewman and frantically wrenched at the wet wood, pulled splintered pieces away and pushed them aside. At last, he shoved a timber that moved enough for Thomas to free himself. The men struggled to shore and lay panting on the rocks.

"My God," gasped Harry. "What happened? Where are William and Arthur?"

Thomas's injuries were assessed by the firemen, and he was transferred to a Portland hospital. Harry stood by helplessly as rescuers made a meticulous search from one end of the fallen trestle to the other. They found the submerged body of conductor Arthur Kinder, who had been crushed by falling timbers.

The search for William Murray was of no avail. If he was pinned inside the cab, they might not recover his body until the bridge debris was cleared away and the train brought to the surface, which would be an arduous and expensive undertaking.

Bystanders watching the rescue efforts spoke in low tones. Some recalled when the original bridge across the Clackamas at Estacada had collapsed under a herd of cattle. The more superstitious among them murmured how death comes in threes. A man was killed during the erection of the railroad bridge, and eight more were killed by the explosion of the donkey engine during the construction of the dam. The trestle collapse was the third fatal accident at or near River Mill.

The search continued all that day and night. A professional deep-sea diver explored the depths for two days. The supposition that William's remains were in the cab was proven false.

Workers began removing debris from the collapse. After two weeks, part of the merchandise bound for Estacada was salvaged from only one car, including sacks of flour, cases of hardware and implements, a drag-saw outfit, a case of shoes, glass and woodenware, utensils and a churn.

Another week passed. Removal of the broken wood structure allowed one of the locomotives to be raised, and William's body, which had been pinned under the wreckage, rose to the surface.

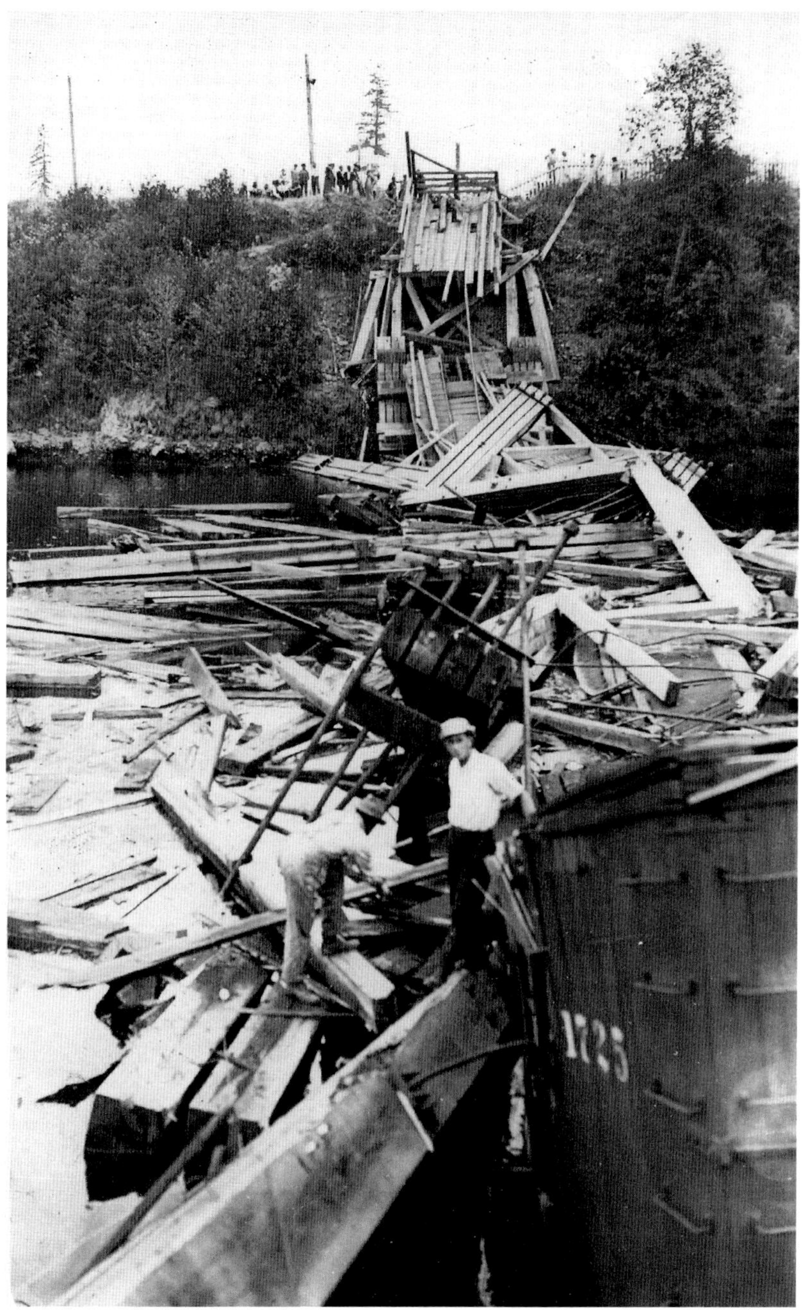

This photo was taken looking toward Springwater shore at 11:00 a.m. on Thursday, July 11, 1918, as the train sank into Estacada Lake. *Courtesy of Jack Reynolds.*

Finally, the last of the debris was lifted from the lake. Bystanders dispersed. Workers went on to other jobs. The railroad announced that it would not rebuild the trestle. In October, the widows of the men who were killed received $7,500 each. Area residents put the tragedy out of their minds.

The turbines in River Mill Dam continued to generate power. On Estacada Lake, all was still but for a slight breeze carrying the scent of Greek oregano.

STEPS

Hurry, hurry, hurry! Step right up to see a marvel of modern technology! A gargantuan undertaking no matter how you look at it.

In 1922, as the construction of the Oak Grove Powerhouse neared completion, PGE installed penstocks—steel pipes encased in concrete—down the mountainside to connect a surge tank to the powerhouse.

There was one problem: the line would have to be inspected periodically for cracks and leaks. A set of concrete steps was poured, rising seemingly vertically up the side of the mountain to the small building containing emergency water shutoff valves. A man was assigned the task of climbing those stairs.

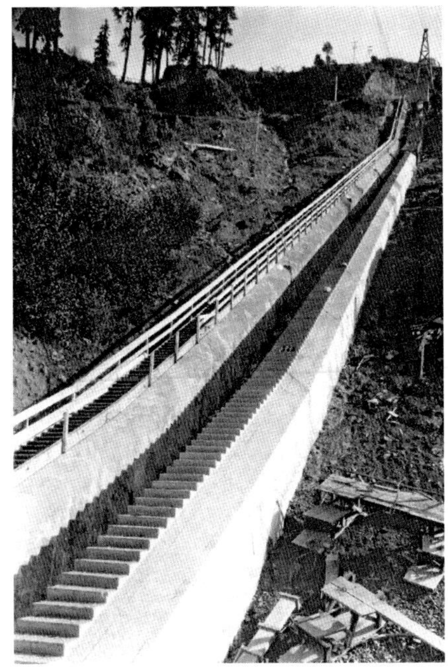

The concrete steps were poured one by one up the steep slope to the top of the mountain. *Courtesy of Jack Reynolds.*

When I first saw the stairs, I was fascinated. When I learned that someone actually climbed them regularly, I was amazed. "How tall are the stairs?" I asked, but no one knew. "How many steps are there?" No one today can remember. A guess was all anyone could offer—about one thousand.

On August 4, 1924, President Calvin Coolidge pressed an electric button on his desk at the White House to officially open the Oak Grove hydroelectric project. Water cascaded through the penstock and down the mountainside, turning the massive wheel inside the turbine to generate twenty-four thousand kilowatts of power.

And the man began climbing the steps.

I recall how, during the artists' day at River Mill Dam, I climbed the five-level circular staircase several times, and I feel my muscles tense even as I remember. As the day progressed and I climbed yet another flight, the fronts of my legs began to burn, my calves started to cramp. As I climbed the staircase for the last time that day, I worried that my legs might not be able to carry me up the final half-dozen steps.

Now I imagine climbing the cement stairs up the mountain. I find it hard to comprehend the trial of the Oak Grove staircase. That man had to climb in all kinds of weather—in blustery rain, bitter wind or driving snow falling so fast that the steps were hidden. Or on an icy morning with feet slipping and sliding. One thousand treacherous steps up and down. It took a remarkably fit person to make it. Who was that man? How many years did he do it? No one remembers.

Today, there is a road part of the way up the hill and a path from the road to the valve area at the top of the penstocks. I wonder if some hardy soul would be willing to take the stairs now.

The steps are long unused, reduced to moss-covered, crumbling concrete. But in my mind's eye, I climb those stairs. To me, they symbolize the determination, stamina and persistence of the men who built Oak Grove.

Hurry, hurry, hurry! See the magnificent powerhouse. Let your eyes rest on the stairs rising up the mountain.

The thought fairly takes my breath away.

Fame

"Ralph Reed was in the washroom when the water came up behind him and washed him out the window." This is one of the anecdotes compiled in a 1979 middle school project featuring snippets of Estacada's olden days. But what is the truth behind this often retold tale?

Four simple wood houses, provided by Portland General Electric for Faraday Dam employees and their families (guaranteeing that personnel would be available for work), sat below what is now Highway 224. A little before 8:00 a.m. on June 15, 1953, mechanic Ralph Reed and another operator left their homes and walked over a cable-strung footbridge to the powerhouse on the opposite side of the Clackamas River.

After Ralph finished some mechanical adjustments, he headed to the washroom to clean up. That was when he saw water leaking from the casing on one of the draft tubes that carried pressurized water to turn the turbines. Ralph ducked into the washroom in the back side of the plant just as the draft tube ruptured, blasting out a triangular hole twenty inches on each side in the cast-iron casing.

According to chief operator Dan Swanson, the blast shoved a huge ceiling crane against the far wall, cracking the wall and causing part of it to disintegrate. A torrent of water shot through the big doors at the end of the powerhouse, taking with it the small patch of lawn where employees often rested.

Within a minute, more than three feet of water covered the floor. A minute later, it was nearing six feet. Undoubtedly, this took Ralph by surprise and forced him to escape. Retired supervisor Bob Brown conjectured that Reed, if caught in the washroom, most likely just waded through the door to the outside to reach the bridge behind the plant and climb to safety.

Chief operator Harold Hoygaard was at the controls. When he heard the explosion and witnessed water spewing into the room, he bravely remained at the switchboard, shutting the turbines off one by one and pulling all the main switches until the plant was safely shut down.

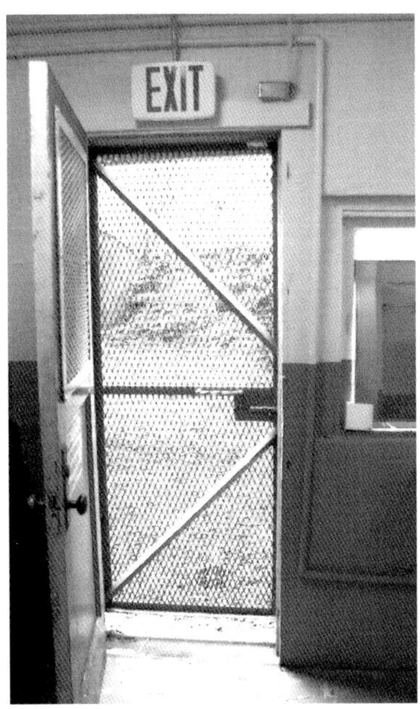

The rising water carried Ralph Reed to safety through this door, which, thankfully, was open at the time. *Author's collection.*

Cap Simpson, who was overseeing a crew painting Bob Brown's house, quickly perceived what was happening and ordered his men to run upstream and close the head gate at the diversion dam to cut off the feed to the powerhouse forebay.

The historical archives of Portland General Electric describe the events of this extraordinary occurrence and report Hoygaard's heroic actions. Strangely, there is no mention of Ralph Reed in the archives.

But after nearly fifty years, people still chuckle as they repeat the popular, most certainly exaggerated retelling of the event: "Ralph Reed was in the washroom when the water came up behind him and washed him out the window!"

Such is the fickleness of fame.

IMPRESSION

Artists create from their impressions of chosen subjects. As a writer, so do I.

When I looked up from the winding road that ended at the bottom of the North Fork Dam, my first impression was…"boring!"

Of course, those who were in the art project had been warned that this dam would be vastly different from the other dams we had visited in past years. In this case, the generators are located on the powerhouse roof and the instruments are inside, underground. The bridge on top of the dam provides a walkway stretching from one side of the Clackamas River to the other. Except for a short distance where we could walk, it is restricted to authorized personnel.

What struck me was the absence of artistic architectural touches. This dam is all business. It was designed with one thing in mind: hold back water and generate power. In the construction of this dam, there was no time for anything that did not contribute to that purpose.

The buildings housing the turbines at River Mill, Oak Grove and Faraday are replete with cantilevered windows, decorative cornices above the doors, majestic and interesting passages and walkways and an open area that resembles a king's throne room with a generator in the place of honor.

The engineers who planned those other dams combined function with art. It was a joy for me to wander through or simply sit inside and absorb the sights and the sound of the huge generators in their settings. Every place I explored held a new surprise.

The men who built these dams were skilled workmen, spending long hours at backbreaking labor. They returned to their homes to rest up for the following day's demands.

Not so with North Fork. These men, many of whom were staying at McRae's Motel, descended on the Estacada taverns and bars, where they stayed until closing time nearly every working night. They were involved in brawls to the point that Police Chief Jim Bardon took them all into custody. He said he came to know them all by name, as he regularly arrested as many as eight at a time over the course of the year the dam was being built.

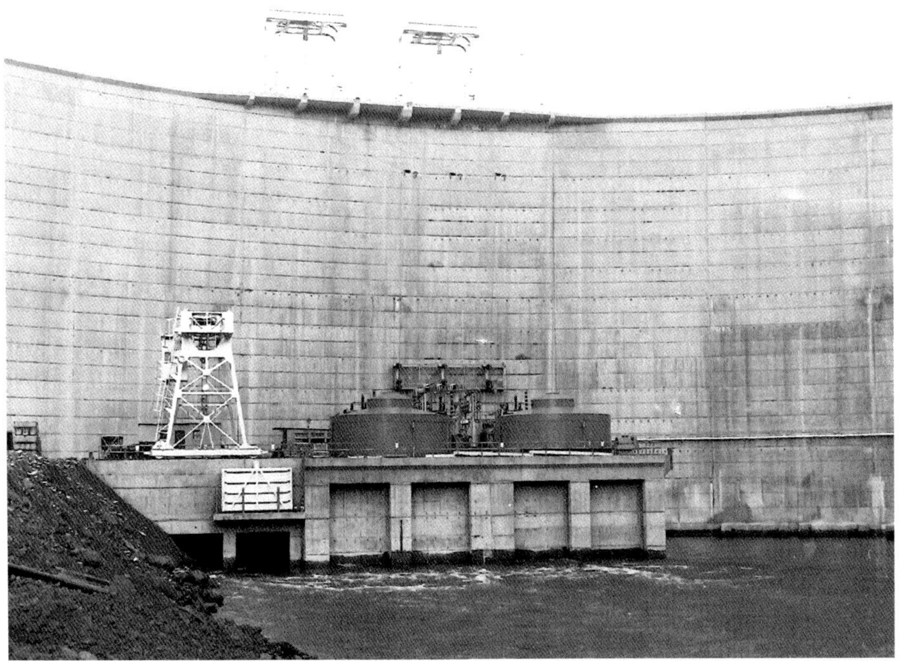

North Fork Dam, constructed in 1957, was the last dam that Portland General Electric built across the Clackamas River. *Author's collection.*

My curiosity is easily piqued. Why were these workers so rowdy when previous construction workers were not? Was the job uninspiring? Did the design lead to boredom? Would they have been less likely to let off steam if their day's work had included an avenue for artistic creativity? We must all release pent-up juices somehow.

According to PGE, this dam is typical of the contemporary hydroelectric projects built in the mid-twentieth century and reflects the architectural style of that period.

The North Fork Dam is a thin arch dam, constructed from huge cement blocks placed side by side from one bank of the river to the other. Layer upon monotonous layer was put into position until the desired height was reached. It is massive. It is forbidding. It is ugly.

But it is imposing. It is mighty. It is efficient. It is the epitome of function. Despite its lack of artistry, it does leave a lasting impression.

3
Uniquely Us

Nailed

In rural areas, community members looked out for and protected one another, a characteristic common in people used to doing what needed to be done. Violet Tucker Heiple related a perfect example of this commitment. One day, she was riding with David Closner in his Model T Ford. They were close to Springwater when David drove across a bridge. Immediately, one of the tires went flat.

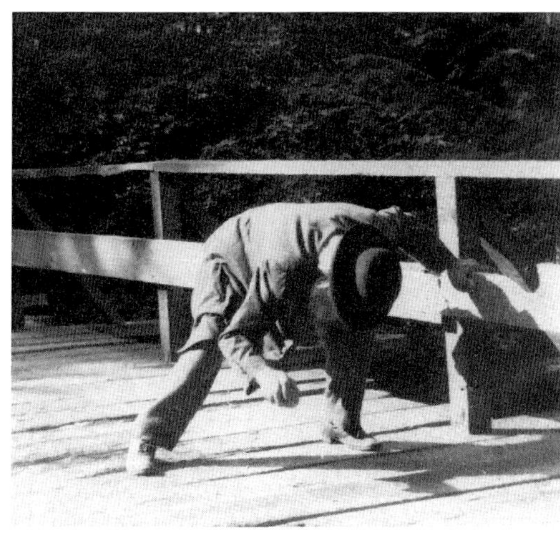

David Closner on the bridge, looking for the nail that punctured the tire on his automobile. *Courtesy of Nancy Tedrow.*

David climbed out of the car, removed the tire and replaced it with the spare. He searched for the cause of the puncture, which proved to be a nail protruding from the deck of the bridge. He drove home, picked up a hammer and took it back to the bridge, where he hammered down the nail so no one else would get a flat.

ARTIST WITH THE GRAVEL

Families pass on items of value. Some hand down recipes. Others bequeath an ancestor's jewelry. For two generations, when their kids bought their first home, residents of the Estacada area pointed their children toward Tom Marlowe, who drove a gravel truck for Estacada Rock Products. When I purchased my house outside Estacada, the seller gave me a packet containing appliance warranties, pump directions and a note: "When you need gravel call Estacada Rock, but request that Tom Marlowe bring it. He's an artist."

Tom began his career in the U.S. Marine Corps, where he attended truck-driving school. When he returned to civilian life, he spent four summers working in Alaska and then drove for a local rock company after returning to Oregon.

Finally, he joined Estacada Rock Products, where he worked for the next twenty-five-plus years. He said it was a nice place to work, with good people to work for. They gave him full benefits and a paid retirement plan. Tom lived in Estacada; working close to home was an added benefit.

Tom's favorite truck was no. 21, a 1995 twelve-yard Western Star equipped with a drop axle and an eighteen-speed Roadranger transmission. His name was painted on the door, a badge of recognition granted to him by the business at his request. If you wanted gravel laid in near perfection, you asked for Tom by name.

Tom had an instinct for timing. He knew when to let the box down without leaving a pile, especially on a short spread of only six feet, and he knew how to set the chains correctly so the exact amount of gravel passed smoothly under the tailgate. No matter the size of the load or the area to be covered, he started up the truck and spread the gravel evenly right to the very end.

His expertise meant that customers did not have to rake and shovel uneven piles of ground rock, a chore if a driver was less careful and less considerate. The buyer's only exercise was writing a check. How did Tom do it? He would modestly explain that it was just lots of practice.

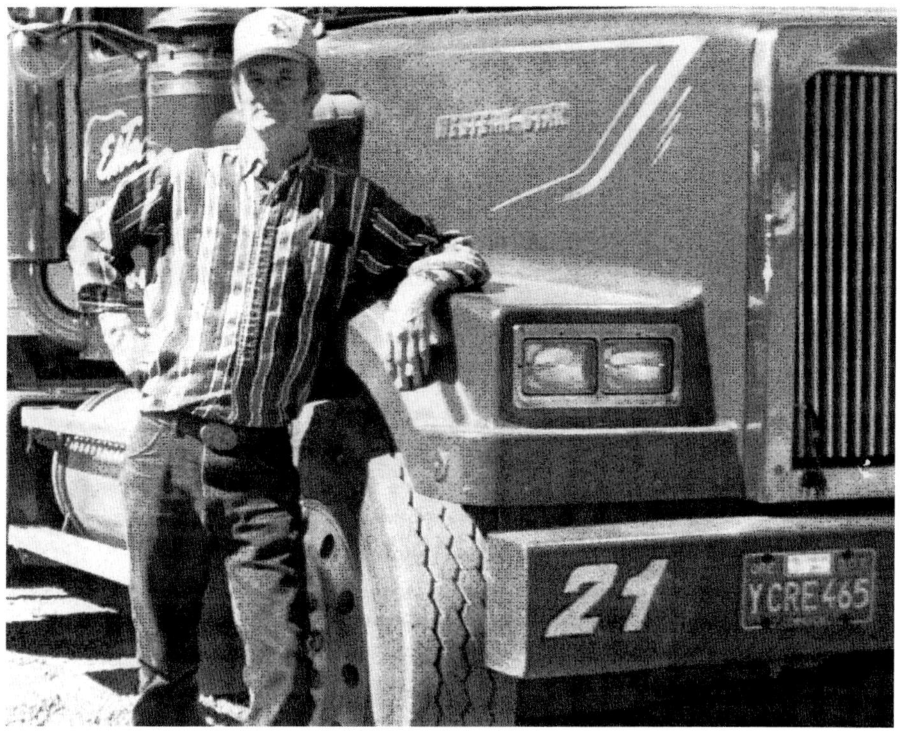

Tom Marlow's name was painted on the door of Estacada Rock Company truck no. 21, which he always drove. *Courtesy of Pam Peterson.*

A residential area could be a booby trap of low power lines. Big tree limbs could break off the radio antennae or damage the box or cab. Stakes in the ground might puncture tires. Concrete sidewalks and drives might crack and break off if the truck came too close to the edge, and a driver's misjudgment could cause a big rig to veer into the wrong area of a yard and sink into a septic tank. Fortunately, Tom knew the secrets to making a fifty-thousand-pound-truck do exactly what he wanted safely.

Competitors in the Oregon Dump Truck Association truck rodeo were judged on their ability to park, handle a variety of obstacles, maneuver through tight spots and drive through cones in various patterns. In the toughest test of the contest, a driver had to remove the tires on the passenger side of the vehicle between two narrow lines of soda cans with tennis balls balanced on top of the lids, without knocking the balls off. The talented Tom Marlowe emerged with a first place trophy. This was no surprise to his employers, who considered him the best driver in the state.

Tom's most valuable attribute was his consideration for the customers. He arrived on schedule, listened to what they wanted and did the job the way they asked him to do it. This attitude helped establish his reputation over the years. If he was busy with a big project, his loyal customers would wait. When he took a vacation, he was booked out two weeks by the time he returned. Long after he retired, no driver was able to match his reputation.

Tom passed away years ago, but if his name is mentioned to any of his customers, they will speak with reverence about his expertise: "Tom Marlowe was an artist with the gravel."

I'll Drive

Glen Wolcott drove log trucks for years, navigating steep grades and hairpin turns. After he retired, if he wanted groceries or other supplies, he drove his car down Squaw Mountain to the store in town, or over to Sandy, or even into Clackamas.

When, in his eighties, he learned that his Oregon driver's license would not be renewed, he was down in the dumps. Then he arrived at a solution, which he related to a neighbor.

"You don't need a license to drive a tractor," Glen said. "So if I need something from town, I'll just drive down on my tractor." When the neighbor asked what would happen if one of the local sheriff's deputies stopped him, Glen had a ready answer. "I'll just tell him I'm going to my field."

Witch Hazel

Ray Miller had the gift. He had used it on his own property, but it was not until late in his life that others become aware of it. He was in his early nineties when he left his farm to visit with his fellow farmers. One day, he was over in the Highland District where a friend was drilling a well. Feeling something peculiar, he called to his friend, "You're drilling in the wrong place. It's over here where I'm standing."

Skeptical, the man shrugged the comment off. But after Ray left, it rolled around in the man's brain. He moved his drilling rig to the spot where Ray had stood and, to his amazement, struck water.

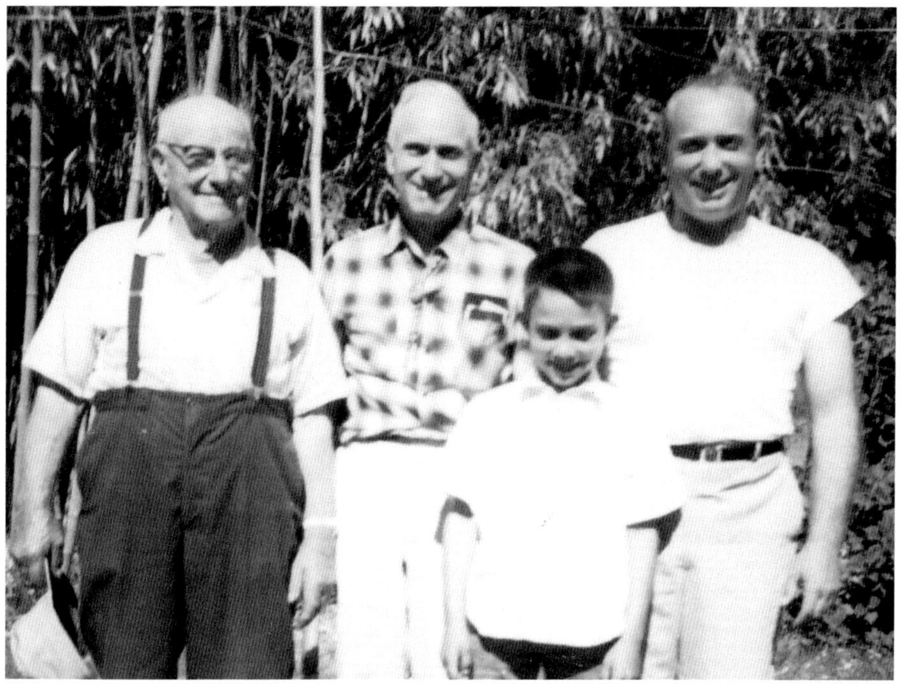

Ray Miller, looking younger than his ninety years, poses with nephew and namesake Ray (*left*), Ray's son Don (*right*) and Don's son David (*front*). *Courtesy of Joanne Jaggers.*

It took only once for word to get around. Soon, a farmer in Redland called Ray to see if he could help find water for a new well on his place. Ray arrived with a forked hazel wood stick about a foot long. Taking the stick by both hands, he held the fork so that the main part of the stick pointed straight up in the air.

Ray walked back and forth until the stick inexplicably dipped down, pointing to the ground. Marking the spot, he continued to walk the property, and twice more the stick pointed down. The farmer dug wells on each spot and found three strong veins of water. Two of them produced 133 gallons per minute.

Another farmer asked for Ray's help, and then another. Each time, Ray was successful. Eagle Creek School needed a well, and Ray found it. It was not long before he became known for his mysterious power around subterranean water.

Starting in 1960, and for the next ten years, he traveled as far as eastern Oregon to help farmers pick the right spot for their wells. If they drilled at the exact spot Ray marked, they always hit water. When asked, Ray said he had no idea what made it work but guessed that the power might have something to do with electrical currents.

The one thing he knew, he said, was that when he hit a vein of underground water, he could not resist the strong pull on the stick. "Sometimes, the power is so strong that it can peel the bark off in my hand." Other people trying to hang on to the stick with him verified that it was, indeed, a strong pull over which they had no control.

The term "witching" was coined by early settlers who successfully dowsed for water with a stick from the witch hazel tree. Dowsing has always been a controversial subject. However, despite scientific ridicule, it is practiced all over the world, including in Viola, Oregon, by a man who had the gift.

Destiny

Charles Miller was born in 1836. He and his wife, Louise, came to America from Ulm, Germany, in 1862, settling first in Chicago, Illinois. In 1870, they moved on to Randolph, Kansas, sixty-seven miles from Abilene, where they opened a dry goods store.

This proved to be poor timing. Kansas began experiencing a severe drought and the accompanying dust storms. Wind blew incessantly. Crop failures were so serious in the western counties that the legislature appropriated money for seed and corn, but this did little to reverse the dire situation. Charles Miller generously allowed homesteaders to charge for goods at his store, but when too many of the homesteaders were unable to pay their bills, the Millers were forced to close the store.

Taking what little savings they had left, the family—which included Charles and Louise and their ten children—came to Oregon in 1896 and settled in the town of Viola, the third-largest trading post west of Mount Hood. Charles put money down on a farm and arranged with a man named Harding to buy the Viola Grist Mill. Here he found a calling foretold by the family name—Miller.

Farmers from Sandy, Garfield, Eagle Creek and Highland brought their wheat to the mill in the summer, when they could travel the roads with their teams and buckboards. They left it to be ground by the Millers but took a small amount of flour to tide them over. They returned on horseback in the winter and collected their flour, carrying it home on packhorses. Charles was a good miller, and his business prospered with the help of some of his children.

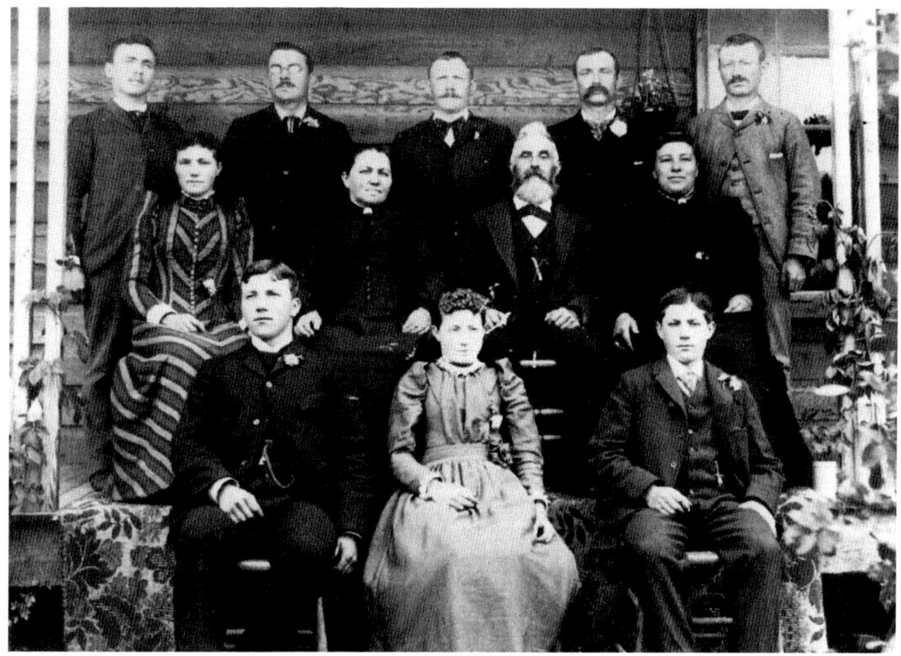

Louise and Charles Miller (*center*) pose for a portrait with their ten children in 1895. *Courtesy of Joanne Jaggers.*

Not all the children stayed in Viola, however. His sons Adolph, Robert and Charles W. were drawn to logging. In 1918, they began operating a logging outfit and mill in the forest up on Fall Creek. Oxen pulled the logs to the mill at Fenton, near the top of Squaw Mountain Road, where the timber was cut and planed into boards. The lumber was then loaded onto an oxen-drawn wagon that traversed a winding, rut-filled dirt road near the top of the mountain to the budding community of George. Most of the barns in the town were built from that wood.

Ray, the youngest son, born on August 9, 1877, stayed in Viola, where he managed his farm until he was in his nineties. In 1960, he became known as a water dowser. In 1921, Charles Miller died in Viola, where he had lived for thirty-five years.

The cement piling and the grist wheel are all that remain of Miller's gristmill on the bank of Clear Creek, but Charles Miller's lasting legacy is the revered Viola School. The school was built on land he sold to the school board—for one dollar.

UP A TREE

During World War II, Americans feared, with good reason, that the Japanese would attack the West Coast by air. The Japanese air force launched helium-filled balloons carrying incendiary devices. The balloons would float across Oregon's borders and explode on impact in the hopes of creating widespread forest fires. One balloon came down in southern Oregon, killing some people attending a church picnic.

On one New Year's Day, Springwater resident Fred Horner saw what looked like a parachute caught at the top of one of his trees. When Fred and his son David cut the tree down, they found a Japanese balloon instead. It measured fifty feet across and had a two-foot-square box that contained a bomb. Fortunately, the bomb had exploded in the air.

The U.S. Army recruited volunteers and trained them as airplane spotters. The volunteers manned towers around the state, including one in Springwater and one in Estacada. One local man's patriotism was so strong that he became a self-appointed spotter on his own land.

He chose one of the tallest trees on his property. He meticulously built a ladder that encircled the tree, winding its way around the trunk like a barber's pole to the topmost branches. He proceeded to build two sturdy platforms; one held supplies he hoisted up by rope, the other allowed him to sit and sleep in the treetop for a couple of days at a time. His months-long sojourn trying to spot enemy planes or incendiary balloons gave him views of the moon, a sky full of stars and the surrounding countryside. It also started his reputation as a "character."

Billy Graham was born in the early 1900s on Fellows Road in Viola. When he was about fifteen years old, he needed money, so he enlisted in the U.S. Army and traveled to Missouri for training. He was assigned to the Seventh Cavalry Regiment, which was responsible for patrolling the U.S.–Mexico border. Rumor has it that Billy Graham trained under a young officer named George S. Patton. Life in the cavalry was ideal for Billy. He became experienced in the care and riding of horses, for which he felt an affinity.

He also felt a rush of patriotism every time he heard the army band play a march by John Philip Sousa. Billy rode in the U.S. Cavalry until his favorable discharge. Following his stint in the service, he returned to Viola, where further exploits added to his reputation. Those who knew him regarded him as "friendly but odd."

Billy's financial security was built, at least in part, by spending his pay from the cavalry on stock in "Ma Bell," as people referred to Bell Telephone

Company. Distrustful of banks, he either hid his money in mason jars and stashed it between the walls of his house or buried it on his property. This eccentricity became a common subject of conversation among the townspeople. After his death, many men came to his farm to dig where they believed the money Billy had buried was located. None was ever found.

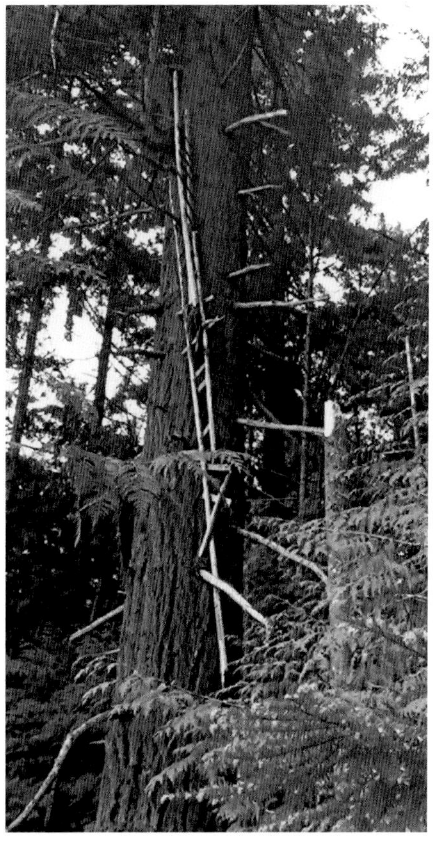

Billy Graham's ladder curved up and around the tree to the platform at the top, where he looked for enemy airplanes. *Courtesy of Mike Misely.*

Billy lived in a two-story house with lap siding built on top of a basement where, in the custom of European farms, his livestock lived. He raised cattle and smelly goats with thick horns that curled backward in a complete circle across their necks. He had horses and mules, always white, both of which he rode. If animals died, Billy piled dirt on them rather than digging a hole.

Billy favored long-legged horses. For years, he rode a tall white horse named Crown that had one blue eye. He made the horse's bit from a big nail, a talent he had learned while in the cavalry.

Billy traveled everywhere on horseback. He delivered mail to Springwater and Viola between 1920 and 1931. He rode Crown to Woodburn, where he worked at the auction house as a "shoo shoo" guy, herding the livestock from the pens to the auction area.

There were no steps leading up to the front porch of Billy's house—he preferred to jump the four feet up from the ground. A lifelong bachelor, he lived on the main floor, where a barrel stove augmented the heat rising from the bodies of the animals underneath. He never closed the stove's door, preferring to keep it open like a fireplace. One window was always open, so he could push the timber for the wood stove in from the outside. He slept on a bed in front of the stove.

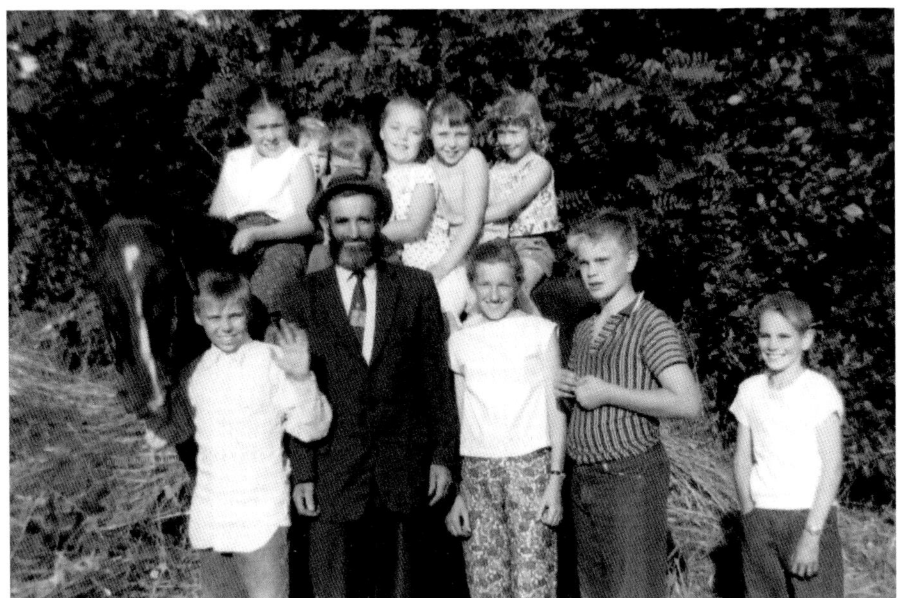

Above: Children were attracted by Billy Graham's personality, delighting in listening to his stories and in riding his horses. *Courtesy of Mike Misely*.

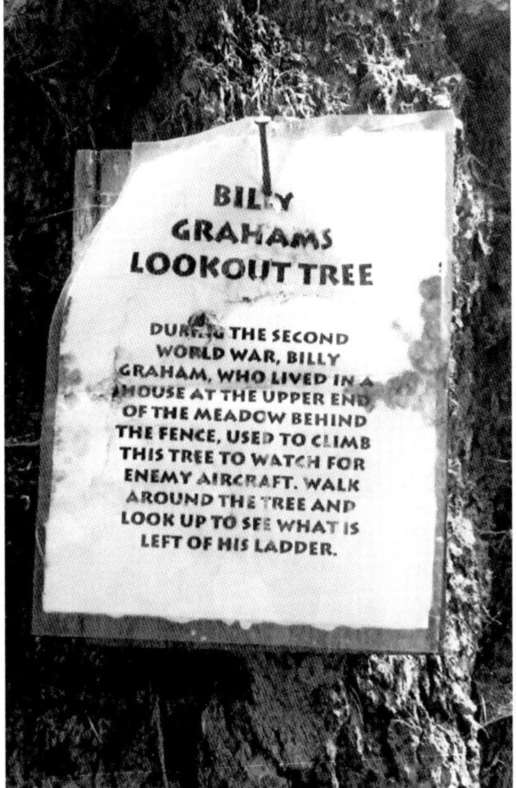

Right: Billy Graham's followers tacked this laminated paper copy to the tree to replace the plaque that was stolen. *Courtesy of Mike Misely*.

He was a talented musician, favoring marches like "The Stars and Stripes Forever," which he pounded out with gusto on the piano in his front room. He also treated guests to renditions on the fiddle. Occasionally, he put on his coonskin cap and hitchhiked into Portland, where he played his fiddle to entertain the men at Bologna Joe's, a shelter for the homeless near the Burnside Bridge. He had a good voice, too. The Highland Quartet he sang with made at least one 78 rpm vinyl record of spiritual songs, such as "Take Up the Cross," "This World Is Not My Home" and "Glory."

Billy's 133 acres gained fame as the Graham Ranch, which led to a bit of excitement in 1966. A couple of convicted murderers broke out of the Oregon state prison and showed up at Billy's place, asking if they could stay there for a spell. He may or may not have known they were convicts, but he said they could. They stayed a couple of months with Billy until the police traced them to his place. The police and the convicts shot it out in the pasture among the cows. Billy wasn't hurt. After it was over, the police asked him why he harbored two criminals. Billy said, "I don't know what they did to you, but they didn't do anything to me."

By the time Billy died in 2000, his reputation as a "character" was well earned. He was buried in Highland. Following his death, a commemorative plaque was attached to one of the trees on his ranch.

His niece Hazel Graham inherited all his land and fortune, but hooligans squatting in his house caused it to catch fire and burn to the ground. She sold the property, which became overgrown with trees and brush so thick that his famous spotting tree could be found only by a determined hiker. The commemorative plaque was stolen. Like so many goings-on in the past, all that is left are the stories.

Searching the Sky

During World War II, America gathered its forces to protect the homeland. In Oregon, the federal government built watchtowers, manned by volunteers who would search the sky at night and immediately report aircraft sightings to the military. Spotters were given a blue armband with gold embroidery, identifying them as observers for the U.S. Army Air Force.

One observation tower was built in Garfield at the northeast corner of Currin Road. Another was built next to the Red & White Store on Springwater Road. Anyone over the age of twelve could volunteer for the

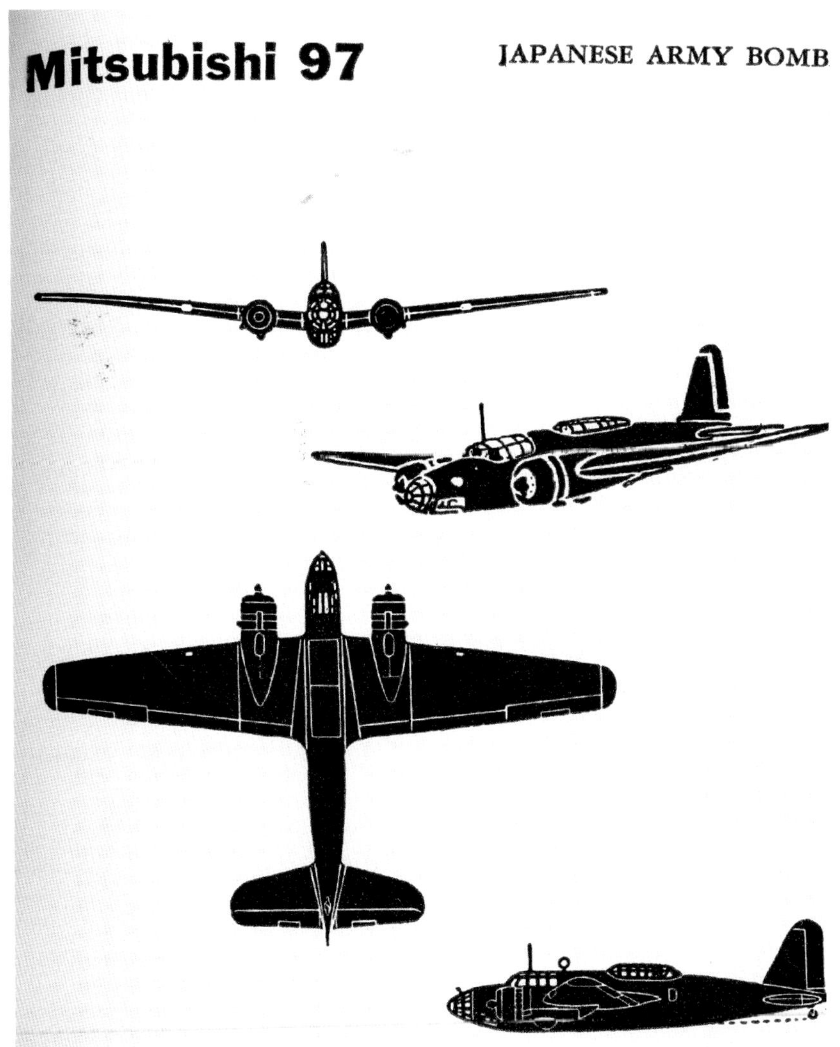

Silhouettes of Japanese aircraft from the training manual *Identification of Aircraft* that volunteer observers had to memorize. *Courtesy of Wilma Guttridge.*

Ground Observer Corps, but anyone who was interested first had to undergo intensive training. Students attended classes from 8:00 p.m. to 10:00 p.m. twice a week for three weeks.

The training manual *Identification of Aircraft* was more than one hundred pages long. The future observers had to memorize the shapes of bombers, fighters, observation planes, trainers, transports and seaplanes. To graduate, they had to demonstrate that they could identify all American and foreign aircraft by the airplanes' silhouette in the night sky. After completing the course, twelve-year-old Wilma Guttridge amassed an astounding 254 hours as a member of the Aircraft Warning System.

SHARPSHOOTER

In 1948, you might not have seen a firing range inside a high school in an average Oregon town. But Estacada has always been different.

As an option to regular studies, students could sign up for a club to fill one of their class periods. Clubs provided an opportunity for students to undertake hands-on projects that expanded their knowledge in subjects they found particularly interesting. Choices included the Science Club, Drama Club and Glee Club. As she entered her senior year, Ruth Reynolds, needing to fill in one more class period, chose the Hobby Club.

Principal Howard Horner, the new club's faculty advisor, suggested developing handicrafts, which failed to excite the thirteen boys. Since they outnumbered the four girls, they voted for gun safety. This did not seem an odd request. After all, this was the country, and there was probably a firearm in every home.

Horner agreed to find a shooting range location by spring. In the meantime, club members decided to start working with leather and entered into projects with equal enthusiasm. Some boys made billfolds. Most students made a pair of moccasins, the girls choosing white leather and the boys brown. During winter, they moved on to the art of tying flies for fishing. When spring arrived, Mr. Horner introduced the project they had waited for: gun safety.

The first lesson outlined the ten rules:

1. *Keep your gun unloaded until you intend to use it.*
2. *Always treat your gun as if it is loaded.*
3. *Do not point the muzzle at anything you do not intend to shoot.*
4. *Don't rely on your gun's "safety" to prevent it from firing.*
5. *Keep your finger off the trigger until you are ready to shoot.*
6. *Be sure of your target, including what is beyond it.*
7. *Be sure the barrel is free of obstructions before loading or shooting.*
8. *Use correct ammunition.*

9. If your gun fails to fire when the trigger is pulled, handle with care!
10. Be aware of your surroundings so you do not trip or lose your balance and accidentally point and/or fire the gun at anyone or anything.

After students committed the rules to memory, they learned how to clean and care for a gun and were shown the various positions from which to shoot.

At last, it was time for the hands-on project, and it was a marvelous surprise. Principal Horner had transformed the cement area underneath the school auditorium into a private rifle range. Stacks of straw bales lined the walls. Targets were pinned to the thick wall of bales at the front of the room. Horner invited participants to bring their guns to school to use on target-practice days. The room, with guns inside, was locked with a key, which Horner kept.

Ruth Reynolds borrowed the .22-caliber rifle owned by her fiancé, John Lazott. With practice, she became an excellent shooter. Her ability was put to the test a few weeks after she and John married on June 12, 1948. The menfolk were sitting outdoors, and the women visited inside.

John's father entered the living room, took his .22 from the gun cabinet and asked Ruth to come outside. He handed her the rifle and one bullet and said, "I bet you can't hit the pigeon over there on that barn." John had been telling his relatives that his new wife was good with a gun, not bothering to add that she had taken the gun safety and target shooting class at the high school.

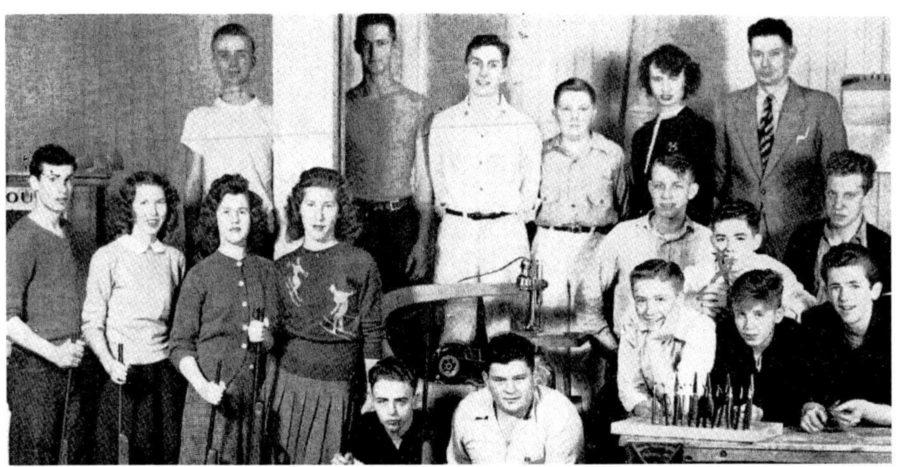

Ruth Lazott (*front row, third from left*) held her .22 rifle for the 1948 yearbook picture of the Hobby Club. *Courtesy of Ruth Lazott.*

All eyes were on her. She was a mite embarrassed—she was just getting to know these grown men—but she loaded the gun with the single bullet, raised the rifle, leaned against the post of the porch, steadied the butt of the gun against her right shoulder, sighted down the barrel and pulled the trigger.

The men began to cheer, but Ruth's new father-in-law said, "No, she missed it." John jumped up, ran across the road to the neighbor's, went behind the barn, found the pigeon and brought it back. Mr. Lazott said, "Well, I'll be darned. Where did you learn to be such a good shot?"

Although she felt bad about taking the bird's life, her participation in the high school gun club had paid off. Her husband was proud of her, and so was his dad. For years after that, whenever the Lazotts got together, her father-in-law would regale everyone with the story of Ruth hitting her target "with one shot!"

Did students walking along the upstairs halls of Estacada High School in 1948 hear the practice rifle shots? No one complained. Was a gun safety club included in curriculums anywhere else in the state? It was never publicized. Did any other Oregon high school create a firing range inside a cement room underneath the school auditorium? Maybe not. But Estacada is—and always has been—different.

Till

Leroy Till Forman, the youngest of three boys, was born in 1920 in a house on the east side of Highway 224, just north of the intersection with Amisigger Road. His father named him after Till Taylor, the sheriff of Pendleton, Oregon, who had met his demise that same year. Till Taylor was, according to Forman, "the last of the Wyatt Earps."

It seems that a convict had escaped from the prison in Pendleton, and a posse led by Taylor set out to capture the fugitive. Till Taylor believed in handling things without bloodshed and so he did not carry a gun. Unfortunately, the convict did have a gun and promptly shot Taylor.

Till Forman's grandfather George Forman had come to Barton from Minnesota. He bought 150 acres of land for $800 and established the Rose Hill Farm in 1882. The sign George placed that year is still in front of the house, now hidden by the arborvitae.

Till's father was named George, too. George Jr. was working as a ranch foreman out at The Dalles when he met his future wife, Minnie Longren, the ranch's cook. They were married in 1906 and came back to the farm at Barton.

George Jr. cleared the land of its many big trees. He raised grain and had ten head of Guernsey cows, four or five horses, a herd of sheep and hogs. The hogs were slaughtered two to three times a year. He sold the cream from the cows to a creamery, whose truck picked up the five-gallon cans at the house. He never sold the milk. Instead, he fed it back to the stock.

In 1910, George Jr. built a beautiful new house to replace the property's original home. The new house was lit and fueled by carbide gas, now known as acetylene. Carbides are colorless crystals that resemble rock salt. George Jr. himself made their gas by placing carbides in a covered hole behind the house and adding a specified amount of water. This combination created a gas with pressure on the line. The line led into the house to lighting fixtures and various appliances.

Mrs. Forman had a gas-driven washing machine. The appliance was used to shuck corn, except when she needed to wash clothes.

All children played on the single-lane dirt road in front of the house, out by the mailbox. But they lost their playground in 1925 when the road was paved and more and more people started driving by. Paving also brought electricity and, with it, electric lights that replaced the carbide lights. Mrs. Forman got a new washing machine and a refrigerator, and she traded in the wood cook stove for a new electric one.

George Forman Jr. never used a power milk separator. He always used the one with a big hand crank and three spouts. The telephone in the kitchen had to be cranked to reach the operator, who would connect them to another phone. Their phone number was 2365.

On some days, Till wandered down to a mill Mr. Burkhardt owned at Barton, downstream on Deep Creek. Till treasured a flour sack he had saved from the mill, with words printed in blue, yellow and pink: "Barton Roller Mills." Below the name was a picture of a pretty woman from her hair to her neckline, with the words "Ladies Choice." The rest of the sack read: "Patent. Flour Manufactured by C.S. Burkhardt, Manager. Barton, Oregon." In tiny letters at the bottom were the words "W.C. Noon Bag Co. Portland, Ore."

The Barton Store, with its big wood porch across the front, was about one-half mile toward Portland. It was always a convenience store, carrying packaged and canned goods. The store belonged to Harvey Gibson. He later sold it to his son-in-law, whose last name was Harvey.

The creek that runs through the property behind the Forman house had salmon that came up from Deep Creek. The fish trying to jump up the six-foot-high dam at the mill were so thick that people used just about anything to snag them. The fish began disappearing in the 1960s, when the Department of Environmental Quality allowed East County Sand and Gravel to pump waste into the creek upstream from Forman's land. Eventually, the DEQ fined the company twenty-five dollars and shut it down, but the salmon never came back.

Before World War II, when the railroad ran up the Clackamas and up Deep Creek, a man named Tuggle took board and room at the Forman house. His job was to inspect the axles on the wheels of the train cars.

Across the road, only one-half mile down the road toward Estacada, was a cabin that housed the first Barton School in 1882. George Jr. attended that one-room school, where Myrtle Griffith taught all eight grades. A second school was built in the early 1900s but was dismantled in 1925.

Till Forman attended the third school, which was built on the same ground as the other two. This was a two-story building with a full basement where the children could play. The main floor had folding doors down the middle that could be closed to form two separate classrooms. Two teachers taught there, one for grades first through fourth and the other for grades fifth through eighth.

Young Till was paid five dollars a month to maintain the school. He cleaned the blackboards, emptied wastebaskets, swept floors and cleaned the bathrooms. He even split the wood for the furnace. He was amazed when the man they hired to replace him earned fifty dollars a month, which was quite an improvement over Till's wage.

To earn some extra money, Till picked apples and sold them to the Barton store, delivering them on a sled pulled by a pony. His older brothers Ray, born in 1911, and Victor, born in 1913, watched him and got an idea: they started a hauling business. The motor vehicle department issued them special plates that read "For Hire."

After high school, Till worked for W.C. Field & Company in Portland for $200 a month. After graduation, he attended Oregon State College from 1938 to 1942. He wanted to study business, but there was no business department as such, so he enrolled in the secretarial courses, learning typing, shorthand and bookkeeping.

Uncle Sam came calling in 1942, and Till was drafted as a second lieutenant. He spent four years in military training, first in Little Rock, Arkansas, then on maneuvers in Louisiana. He was a member of the 507th Military Infantry paratroopers. He was stationed in Alliance, Nebraska, in 1943 and was then sent to train in Ireland and England, where he made thirty-five successful parachute jumps.

Then came the army's push to reclaim France from Germany. Paratroopers were part of the operation, and Till jumped into Normandy at 1:30 a.m. on D-Day, June 6, 1945. Nine hundred planes were attached to the 82nd Airborne, part of the 101st Airborne. The paratroopers of the 507th Military Infantry were supposed to jump close together and take three bridges in the little town of LaFierre to prevent the Germans from sending reinforcements when the troops stormed the beaches. Forty men jumped first, to guide the paratroopers in, but only one of them hit the correct area. As a result, the paratroopers ended up scattered over forty miles.

Till and some of his comrades landed in the middle of twenty acres of land bordering the Saint Meinrad River. Deep ditches bordered the fields so water could drain and be carried to the river, but the Germans had closed the tide boxes; the river backed up and covered the fields with three feet of water. When the paratroopers tried to wade out, they stepped into ten feet of water in the ditches they could not see. The farmers had not been able to mow their fields, and tall grass floated on the water. But there was no grass floating over the ditches. Till said that, once he figured that out, it was easier to wade out.

Two hundred Americans finally hit the railroad but were caught by German machine guns. The Germans came back with tanks and captured LaFierre.

American troops set out to recapture the town and take the bridges, but in doing so, they lost between three hundred and four hundred men. Till remembered the gruesome sight as soldiers and officers from many different outfits fell one on top of the other. One of the men he served with was whispering information into Till's ear when he was shot full of holes by German machine gun bullets. One of the bullets was a clean shot through Till's leg.

Many years later, Till and some of the other survivors of the battle traveled to LaFierre, where they built a monument to their fallen comrades.

His brothers Ray and Victor had both become loggers, but that did not interest Till. After the war, anyone could buy army surplus trucks. After Till returned home in 1946, he bought his first rig, a Diamond T dual-drive-front single, and started a heavy-construction business. He named the company ELTE, which is the sound of his initials, L.T., based on his full name, Leroy Till.

Till had acquired three or four trucks and some caterpillar tractors when he was recalled to the army and sent to Korea. Soon after he returned home, his father had a stroke and hit his head on the cupboard in the kitchen when he fell. He went into a nursing home, and Till moved back home to be with his mother. His father died in 1956 at the age of eighty-two. His mother died in 1961.

Till continued growing his business, which saw lots of work after his company began working for the Federal Highway Administration in 1990. His brother Ray's son, Wes, took over running the company.

Till was moved by the atrocities of war to which he was witness, but that was a long time ago. When recalling his life, the thing that seemed to touch him most had happened more recently. At the end of our interview, he said wistfully, "The coyotes got my border collie last summer. He was on my side of the fence. It was the first time in my life that coyotes took any of our animals."

PLATTED OUT

Estacada was not the only town that Oregon Water Power & Railway Company (OWP&R) envisioned. After the railroad to Cazadero was completed, the Oregon Water Power Townsite Company thought that families would flock to communities on the railroad line. They heralded the plan as "Barton, Oregon, The New Town on the OWP&R Line." Lots were auctioned off for one hour only. Corner business lots sold for one hundred dollars, and inside lots went for seventy-five dollars. Buyers were required to pay half down, and the balance could be paid at ten dollars per month. Residential lots were fifty dollars for a corner and thirty-five for inside lots. These could be purchased for half down and five dollars a month. Interest was set at 7 percent. There is no record of how many lots were sold, but Barton did not grow into the community OWP&R had hoped.

BADGERS

The National League was formed in 1869, and the sport of baseball quickly became the national pastime. In Barton, the hardworking farmers could relax while cheering on their home-grown Barton Badgers baseball team in 1910.

4
Home

The House on the Hill

If houses could talk, this one would have had a lot to say. It was built on Wilson Hill Road, three miles above Estacada, overlooking Wade Creek around the end of the 1800s.

O.C. Klaetsch lived there with his family while he dammed the creek below the house to form a big pond for the mill he built alongside the creek. He methodically cut the old-growth cedar trees from both sides of the ravine, milled them and sold the lumber.

The trees measured eight to fifteen feet across at the base. Klaetsch cut the stumps ten feet high for three reasons: it was easier than chopping or cutting through the base; the grain at the butt ran in too many and varied directions, making poor lumber; it was always harder to saw at the mill.

Once the trees were gone, Klaetsch moved his family and his mill to other, more prolific forested areas. The City of Estacada temporarily left the dam, using the pond as a water reservoir for the town's residents.

In 1917, John and Hattie Saunders purchased the house upon their arrival to the United States from Canada with their children, Lucile, Ivan and Ruth. The dam had been removed, and the pond was gone.

John used the hillside as pastureland for cows, which grazed among the cedar-tree stumps dotting the hill above the creek. John cut two-foot-high pieces of wood from the stumps to make cedar shakes and firewood.

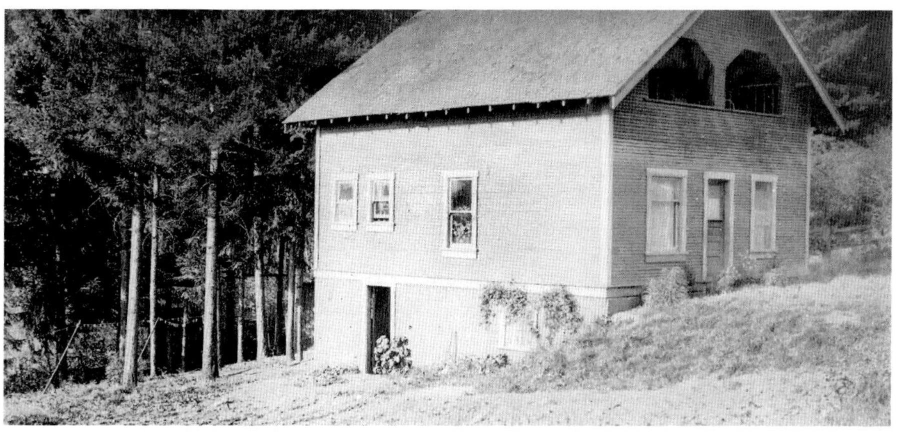

The simple-looking house on Wilson Hill Road. *Courtesy of Barb Hicks.*

In the middle of the hill grew a single clump of Himalaya blackberry that measured about twelve feet across. The Himalaya was rare in those days, so John built a fence around the bushes as a protection from the bovines so his wife could pick the fruit for her delicious blackberry pie.

Their daughter Lucile was married there, and in the 1940s, her children played on the hillside among the cows. The little girls delighted in making fancy hats from the rhubarb in grandmother Hattie's vegetable garden by cutting a leaf, turning it upside down and attaching a bird feather at a jaunty angle on the top.

Close to the now-meandering stream, water and time had caused the old stumps to disintegrate, leaving the rotted-out scalloped edges of the roots standing a few inches high. The circumference of the roots formed areas just large enough for the Saunderses' grandchildren to use as pretend houses. Woe to the child who did not recognize the convoluted roots as indications of the rooms of a house and stepped over them!

Following her husband's death in 1965, Hattie sold the house. It is possible John Bess became the new owner, and he may have lived there into the twenty-first century.

In the 1970s, when Clackamas County renamed many roads to honor original pioneers, Wilson Hill Road was changed to Coupland Road. In 2012, one of the monstrous cedar trees surrounding the old house crashed into the roof during a windstorm. The damage to the house was extensive, requiring its demolition. A mobile home was moved to the spot where the house once stood. It is modern and attractive, but it will never be witness to historic incidents like those seen by the house on Wilson Hill.

Drink Up

Drivers traveling east on Coupland Road may wonder why one of the houses they pass has an unusual "in-and-out" driveway. From the 1940s to the '60s, the home belonged to a colorful guy named "Lucky" Hunter. He was one of the most popular men around because he provided moonshine for the locals.

The driveway allowed folks to drive into the upper entrance, put their money into a jar on a flat rock beside the driveway, drive down the hill and return to pick up a mason jar filled with spirits sitting on the same rock.

Apparently, the thriving business filled a vital need, since the city has no records indicating that there were any raids on the house. Perhaps that accounts for the nickname "Lucky."

Sturdy Home, Sturdy Folks

Halley F. Gibson started H.F. Gibson General Merchandise, Barton's first store. He also built houses, including one for his brother Harvey and a nearly identical one for himself near the store. Sturdy and attractive, two of Halley's houses are in use as family residences more than 120 years later. Although Harvey's home no longer exists, Halley's home stands next to the old-style Barton Store on Highway 224 at Barton Road. The other house can be seen on the east side of Highway 224 at the junction with Amisigger Road.

William Preston "Press" Ferrel and his wife, Nancy Jane, bought one of Halley's houses after they moved to Oregon from Virginia with their one-year-old daughter, Grace. They traveled to Oregon City by train and then by stagecoach to Estacada. In 1903, they arrived in Currinsville, where they knew people who had come to Oregon before them. The Ferrels fell in love with one of Gibson's houses set on forty acres in Barton.

Back home in Virginia, Press had been a bartender, but after the move to Oregon he earned money as a woodsman and later as a night watchman at a mill on the river just below their house. On their farm, he raised cattle and hogs to sell, and he cut and hauled logs to companies in Portland for use as firewood.

Nancy was an extremely talented woman who knitted, crocheted, quilted and sewed all of her children's clothes. The house's handsome wood floors were covered in rugs woven from worn-out clothes, and her handmade sheets and pillowcases were decorated with knitted lace. She was a beekeeper

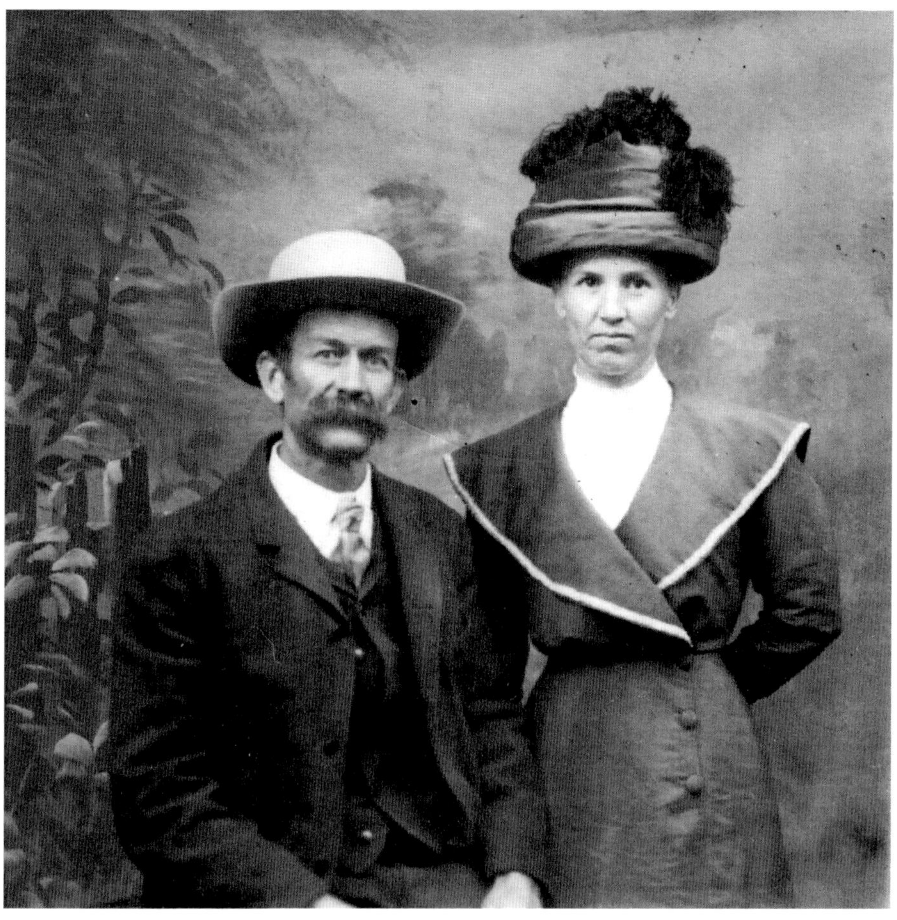

A portrait of Nancy Jane and William Preston "Press" Ferrel that Nancy took before they left Virginia for Oregon. *Courtesy of Ruth Lazott.*

and drove the family's cars (Press did not want to). An expert photographer, she had a darkroom in their home, which accounts for the fact that her descendants own quantities of treasured family photographs.

Press died in 1943, but Nancy was not about to leave the home she loved. She stayed there until 1973, working the farm, taking care of two hundred chickens, milking two cows and raising her own food. Her colorful flower garden bloomed beside the front and side yards, which she mowed with an old push-mower until she was ninety-two years old.

Nancy lived in the home until a year before she died. After her death, the house was rented out, but it was destroyed in a fire caused by either a lighted

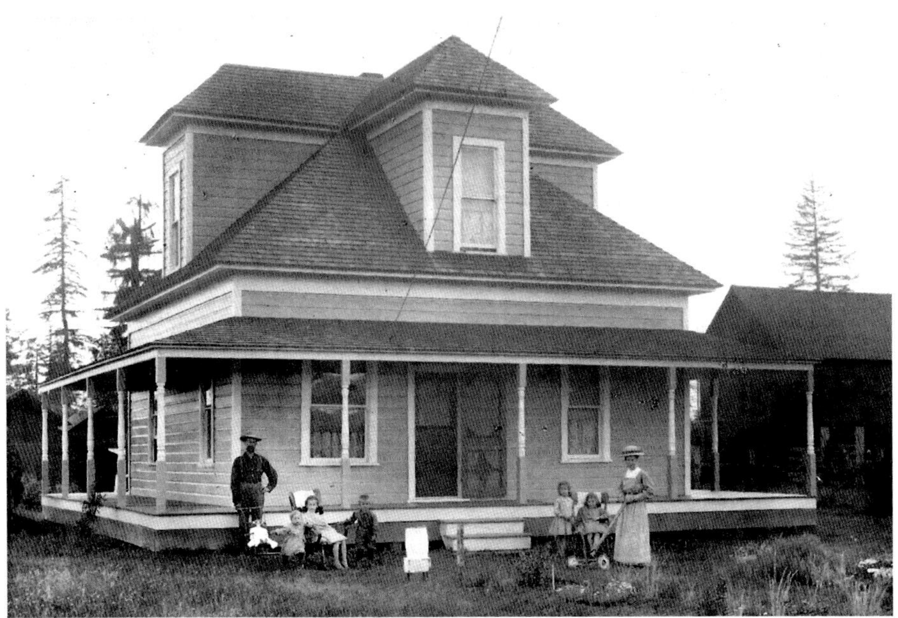

Press, Hugh, Grace, Bill, Edith, Maude and Nancy Ferrel in front of their new home in Barton, built by H.F. Gibson. *Courtesy of Ruth Lazott.*

Christmas tree or a burning cigarette. Although the house the Ferrels loved for all those years is gone, two others in Barton are there for those who want to take a look. Nancy's descendants cherish the photo she took of her family in front of the other house that Halley Gibson built.

BYRD'S ROOST

Iris Byrd was the granddaughter of George Currin, who came to Oregon from Iowa in 1845 and started the town of Currinsville. Iris's parents, George Aschenbrenner and Olive Currin Aschenbrenner, often talked about Currinsville, which was once a busy, going concern with a railroad stop directly across from the store. The town was the center of activity in the area until the Oregon Township Company started Estacada the year before Iris was born. George and Olive recalled that after 1905, the new town was the place to be.

Although her parents settled in Covina, California, Iris and her mother made yearly trips to Currinsville, traveling by train to Portland and then taking the streetcar to Estacada.

All of Iris's cousins, aunts and uncles lived in and around Currinsville. She and her cousins would walk down to the Clackamas River to play. "Oh, we had such fun," she said. "Estacada Park had a stairway that led down the bank to a platform at water level. We just waded out into the river. Nobody ever drowned."

Iris loved being here. She and her mother, who never got over being homesick, wanted her father to sell his orange groves, move to Currinsville and buy a farm. But "he was too smart for that."

Iris studied at the School of Costume Design in Los Angeles and was hired as a costumer for Paramount and Republic movie studios. She remembered being at Paramount the day Will Rogers and Wylie Post were killed when their plane hit a glacier. "We were ready to shoot a scene when word came. We just quit. The studio shut down, and we all went home."

She enjoyed her association with amiable members of the film industry and worked on many movies. Her fondest recollection was of Gene Autry, an extremely nice person and a real gentleman. He often went to her apartment to visit with Iris in the evening. He never made passes, and he would talk about things he wanted to achieve in life. Gene went into the service during World War II. The studio took on Roy Rogers and Dale Evans to replace Gene, but Iris thought they just could not do as well. When Autry left the studio, Iris left, too.

Iris studied real estate and became a realtor. Because traveling by road was too time-consuming, she learned to fly. Iris was a longtime member of the "99 Women Pilots" club, half of whom lived in Washington, the other half in Oregon. In 1975, she purchased an old Piper tri-pacer ("It was a real dog"). When she landed it in Coachella, California, the plane was leaking oil. Bob Byrd, an inspector for the FAA, saw it and grounded Iris. The accidental meeting developed into a romance, and they were married in 1980.

At Iris's urging, the couple flew to Currinsville every summer. One year, they learned that the old Osborne place on five acres was for sale. The land had grown ginseng, but once that venture failed, John Osborne turned it into a filbert orchard. Using her real estate acumen, Iris decided it was a good investment, so they bought it. For a while, Bob and Iris flew up to Estacada for the summer and continued to live in California in the winter, but they eventually moved here for good. This was where Bob died.

Iris was proud of her Currin heritage. For a long time, she took care of the Estacada Museum, which was housed in the city hall. She donated many Currin items, including the Currin Bible, her Grandfather Currin's powder horn, pictures of relatives, their piano and the old wood washing machine she had found in the Osborne filbert orchard.

Iris lived for nearly one hundred years. It had taken a long time for her to return to the homeland of her family, but as Bob once affectionately told her, "The Byrd has come home to roost."

There Is Nothing Like a Coke

The thirty-six-inch-high red chest on the porch of Mike's store sported bold white letters declaring "Drink Coca-Cola. Ice Cold." Nothing was quite as rewarding as dropping a nickel through the slot and then reaching into the icy chest, grabbing the bottle top and moving it down through the zigzag metal tracks that clicked open so you could pull out a tasty cola.

Mike's store was legendary. It belonged to Mikel Matelewski, who had escaped from Latvia in 1914 when Germany took possession of his country and demanded that all males fight in the German army. At the age of seventeen, he left his family behind and immigrated to America. He served in the U.S. Army in World War I and, as a result, qualified for the Homestead Act. He chose acreage up Squaw Mountain Road one hour from Estacada, where he built a store with living quarters in the back.

Mike's store was painted red, white and blue—not out of patriotism, but because the single pump in front of the store sold Standard Oil gasoline and those were the company's colors. A hand pump fed gasoline into the glass dome on top marked with lines indicating gallons. Then gravity brought the gas down from the dome through the hose. As the car's tank filled, the level in the glass dome dropped. In this way, the operator could count the lines on the glass and charge the customer for the gas he took.

Rumor has it that Mike kept a shotgun beside the front door, using it when teenage punks with no money came in for gas and sped off without paying. There is no proof that Mike every hurt anyone, but he reportedly put a hole or two in the trunk of several cars before they disappeared around the corner and down the hill.

Mike, a nice, clean-shaven guy, was friendly, but he had one heck of an accent. Old-timers remember that "he could talk your arm and your leg off if you had a day to listen." By contrast, Mike's wife, Mae, was a quiet woman. They met late in their lives, when Mae, a retired schoolteacher, moved up Squaw Mountain with a friend to a house near the store. Mae never waited on customers, preferring to stay in the back.

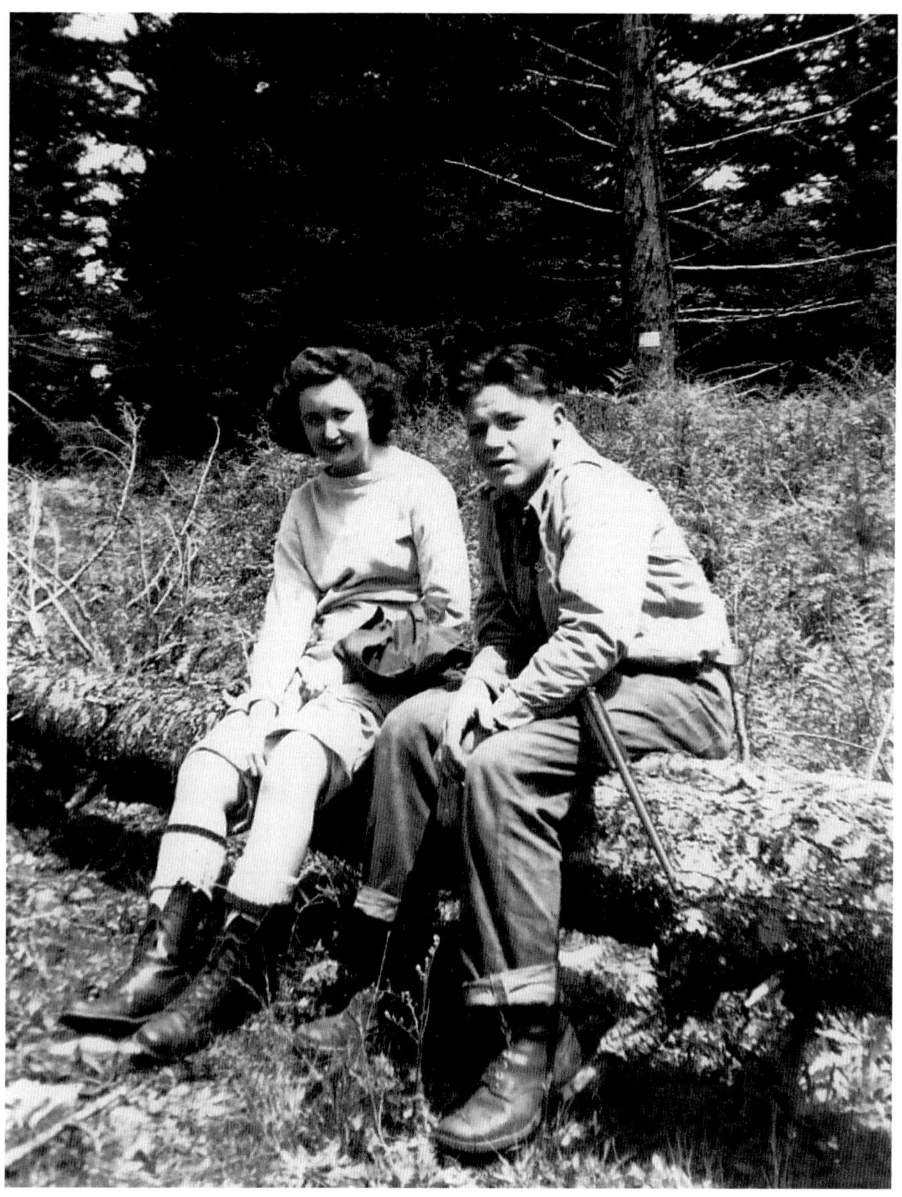

John Poppino and a friend he met after the family moved to the farm up Squaw Mountain Road. *Courtesy of Teri Poppino.*

The store was the center of the community, and Mike was the repository of information, since the locals bought supplies there and stayed to visit. If you wanted to know what was happening, Mike shared the news with gusto.

The store sold bread, coffee, milk, sugar, Corn Flakes, ice cream and other staples. Employees of Squaw Mountain Logging, owned by Anton "Tony" and Eddie Lausmann, stopped in regularly to replenish their supply of cigarettes, snuff and chewing tobacco. The bachelor loggers, one of whom was Ivor Coup of the Coupland Road family, lived in the twelve one-room bunkhouse cabins that Jake Walcott had built in the clearing west of Mike's store. Irwin "Grease Monkey" Sagner, son of Rudy Sagner, Estacada fire chief, lubricated the logging equipment. Eddie worked in the woods with the crews. Tony, the logging manager, lived in a house in a clearing on the right side of the road and worked in the logging office. The cookhouse fed the company's crew as well as other Squaw Mountain loggers. Tony was a musician who entertained the Pacific Logging Congress meetings with "Lausmann's Lousy Loggers Band."

Seven families living on Squaw Mountain relied on Mike for basic supplies, including the Fantons; the Carters; Rollie and Greta Poppino; Bill Dwyer, who had a small sawmill on Bee Creek; and Albert Adlon and his wife, Janet, who was Mae Matelewski's daughter. George Clark lived across the road from Mike's store with his son David. Then there were residents of the Squaw Mountain Ranch Nudist Club and the U.S. Forest Service rangers who periodically stayed in the sixteen- by twenty-foot Fanton Guard Station.

Some people say that members of the Warm Springs Indian tribe came up Squaw Mountain Road once a year on their way to the open ridges where the sweet huckleberries grew. The men and young women rode bareback on ponies, but the old man handled the team pulling the buckboard where the older women sat along with the canvas tents and cooking utensils. They didn't stop at Mike's.

On warm afternoons, the "school bus"—a 1938 one-ton panel truck with a bench in the back—might stop at Mike's on its run between Fanton and Porter so kids could buy a Coke or an ice cream cone. With gnarled hands, Mike personally dipped the ice cream out of the five-gallon tub in the freezer. Mr. Botkin, who contracted to carry school students, owned and drove the bus. Riders claimed he didn't drive too well in the best of times.

A real 1935 school bus replaced the panel truck for "safety reasons." Once Mr. Botkin met a log truck as he drove down the one-way Porter Road. The truck backed up so they could pass, but the old mechanical brakes on the

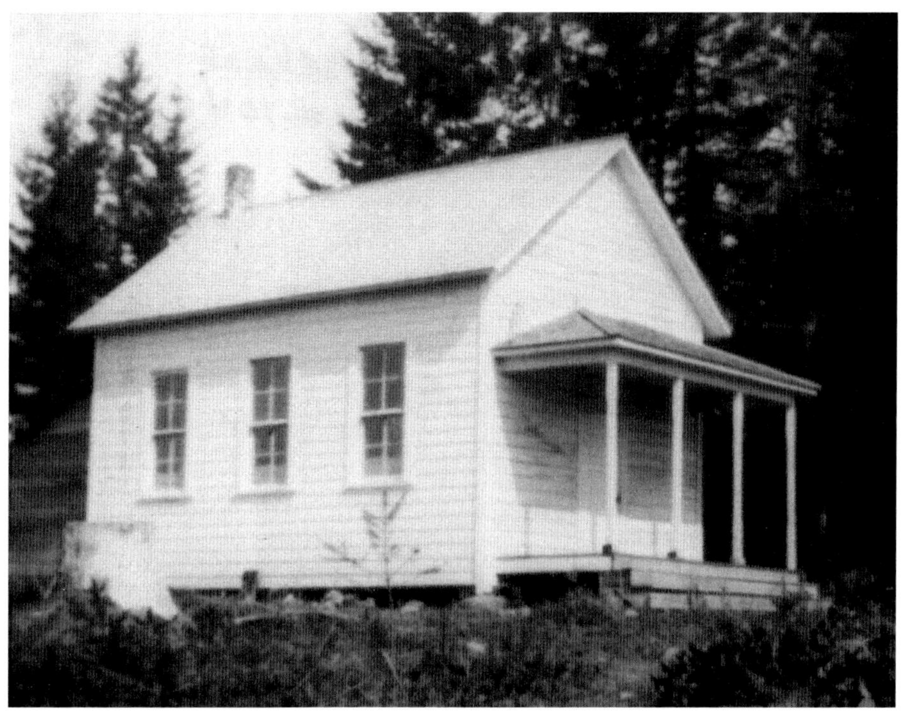

The one-room school at Fanton before Georgia Munch bought it and remodeled it into a house. *Courtesy of Sylvia Bowman.*

bus couldn't stop. As the schoolgirls shrieked and the boys cheered, the bus plowed right into the log truck.

In 1942, a P-39 airplane dove into the hillside about a mile south of Mike's, killing the pilot. Men reaching the wreckage found .50-caliber bullets and a 20-millimeter cannon mounted in the middle of the propeller.

Over time, the area around Mike's store changed. Portland General Electric bought the farmer-owned cooperative Rural Electric Administration lines and began providing power to the residents, to the vexation of the independently minded Squaw Mountain men.

The logging company moved on. Many of its cabins were relocated to Squaw Mountain Ranch up the road. Fanton Guard Station was sold. The new owner moved it a bit and converted it into a home. In 1940, the Fanton family's house was sold to Georgia Munch, who remodeled it and made it her home. When the Fanton School, on the left-hand side of Squaw Mountain Road near the terminus of Fall Creek Road, was closed prior to 1943, Georgia bought that building and remodeled it into a house. Unfortunately, when she moved to the school, the Fanton family house became a party house. Partygoers, who stopped at Mike's for beer and chips, trashed the old house. It eventually caught fire and burned to the ground.

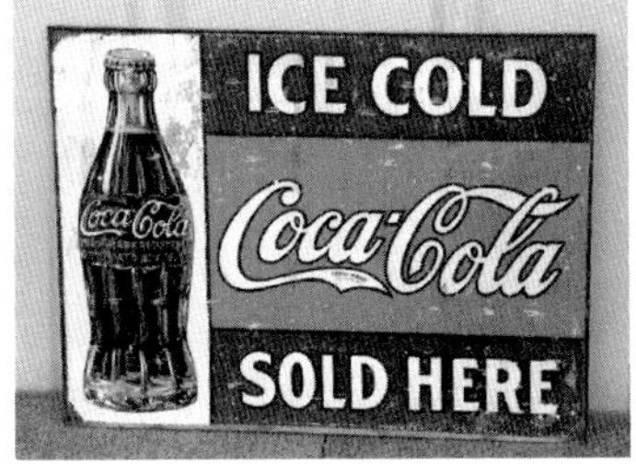

Mike Matelewski probably tacked up advertising signs like this on the front of his store. *Author's collection.*

In 1956, Mike placed an ad in the Estacada newspaper. "Because of my wife's illness, I am closing out my grocery stock and fixtures. Make an offer." After both Mike and Mae died in the late 1950s, Publisher's Paper bought the property from Mae's daughter, leveled Mike's store and logged the 160 acres behind it.

Nearly seventy years later, men and women who as children stopped for a Coke at Mike's store are still nostalgic about the establishment. Over the years, several of the old-timers stopped on the road and walked into the trees and brush in a vain attempt to locate the remains of the store.

Then, in 2015, a local man was exploring Squaw Mountain Road with his metal detector when he happened upon a cement slab off the road. To one side he found a pipe that ran down the slope from what might have been a gasoline tank. Behind the slab in what he presumed to be a trash heap, he unearthed a gold, ornately decorated lipstick case and an ancient Coca-Cola can. Farther down he found several old Coca-Cola bottles that, during the 1930s and 1940s, would have been dispensed from a red ice chest with white writing, typically residing in front of convenience stores and gas stations. The legend of Mike Matelewski's store lives on.

WHAT AN EYEFUL

John Poppino was in the eighth grade when his family moved to the farm near the top of Squaw Mountain Road. His new schoolmates were happy to tell him all about the neighbors. They relished showing him the sign for Squaw Mountain Ranch and passed on stories they had heard about the nudist club.

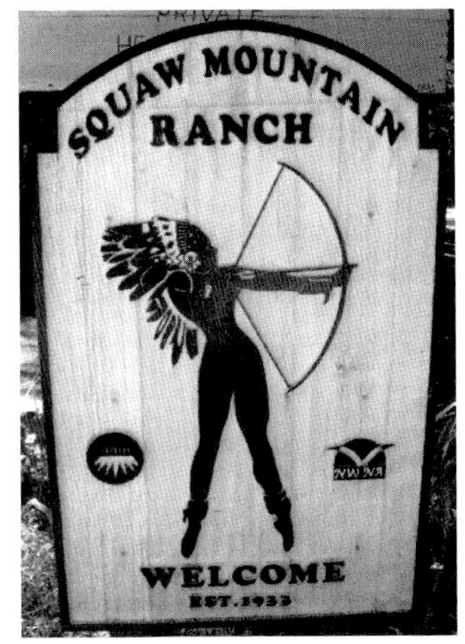

After digesting their tales, his curiosity got the best of him, so John decided to go there and see the camp for himself. He climbed a tree near the fence surrounding the camp, thinking he might catch a distant view of the club members.

He was barely settled on a tree limb when a group of people came into the grassy area beneath him and started playing a volleyball game. There was no escape. John's only recourse was to cling to his perch while the nudists, in all their naked glory, played a very long game.

A weary John Poppino was finally able to climb down. Boy, did he have a colorful story of his own to share with his new friends!

You're Pulling My Leg!

Today, Oregon Fish and Wildlife wages a constant battle against bullfrogs, which are not native to the area. As a matter of sad fact, bullfrogs kill the native frogs. Where did these predators come from? In the Garfield area, a possible explanation dates to the late 1930s.

A man, whose name no one can remember, read about expensive restaurants serving frogs' legs as a delicacy. He got the not-so-bright idea that he would make his fortune by selling frogs' legs to satisfy the appetites of the wealthy. He bought some starter bullfrogs and set up his enterprise on his property on Squaw Mountain Road, about fifty yards below the Porter Road cutoff.

Unhappily, the venture failed to live up to his expectations. He dammed the creek that ran through his property to form a little swampy pond. He enclosed the pond with a flimsy board fence to keep the predators out and the frogs in. Neither of these was successful.

To top it off, his pre-business research was very poor. Since, at that time, there was no such thing as overnight shipping, there was no way to get the legs to the restaurants before they spoiled.

He finally gave up and let all the bullfrogs go. Remnants of his folly can be seen in the decaying wood fence and heard in the overwhelming sound of croaking bullfrogs.

Opposite: The sign at the driveway leading to the nudist club, which has been at the end of Squaw Mountain Road since 1933. *Courtesy of Squaw Mountain Ranch.*

5
That's Entertainment

The Museum of Memorabilia

Some people seem destined from birth for a specific career. Mike Doolittle was one such person.

Mike was born in 1952 in Cottage Grove, Oregon, the third of six children. When he was five years old, his family moved to Estacada. That year, his parents gave their young son a little Red Flyer wagon. They soon feared they had made a big mistake.

Mike loaded his cart with anything he found fascinating and proceeded to drag it home. His mother, Audrey, was dismayed because "what he found was pure junk." She didn't know back then that Mike had an eye for things of value and could spot them among items others threw away.

Mike stored his exciting finds in the garage until his mother said, "Enough!" Then he began smuggling items into his bedroom, and although she didn't like that, Audrey had to admit that the bedroom was always neat and organized. As his collections grew, Mike began stuffing them into the crawl spaces under the neighbors' houses. The interesting rocks he found were added to an increasingly large pile in the yard.

While he was in the fifth grade, one of his junking expeditions yielded a black metal lunch box filled with old keys. One day, his mother received a call from Mrs. Austin, the secretary at the school. "Oh, no," Audrey moaned. "What has Mike done now?" As it turned out, Mike had made his first cash sale—Mrs. Austin wanted to buy the keys for five dollars. Mike ran home with the money safely in his pocket, pleased to have vindication that what he did was actually worth something. Audrey met her young entrepreneur at the door and commented affectionately, "Wipe that grin off your face—right now."

When the family was moving to a new home, it was apparent that Mike couldn't take all his accumulations with him. In a foreshadowing of his business acumen, he came up with an ingenious plan: he invited all the neighborhood children to come to an auction. He gave them each a number cut from paper and instructed them to call out their number when he pointed at them. Regardless of the number called out, Mike would say, "That's the lucky number," "You won" or "That's close enough" and proceed to hand them something from his stack of "junk." One thing he took to the new house was his rock collection, which he used years later as part of a fountain that stood in front of his store.

When Mike was a freshman in high school, he found pieces of a chair tied in a bundle, set out in the alley for the garbage pickup. Mike asked the homeowner if he could have something from his trash heap. The man shook his forefinger at Mike and said sternly, "Go ahead and take it—just don't bring it back."

Mike took it home, but his mother once again said, "Get that junk out of here." Mike asked his ninety-three-year-old neighbor if he could keep the pieces of his find in the man's garage while he tried to fix it. Mr. Kingston, a retired machinist, not only said "Yes" but also took an interest in Mike's project and offered to help reconstruct the chair. They laid the pieces out on a workbench in the garage near the 1937 Chevrolet Mr. Kingston drove downtown for coffee each day.

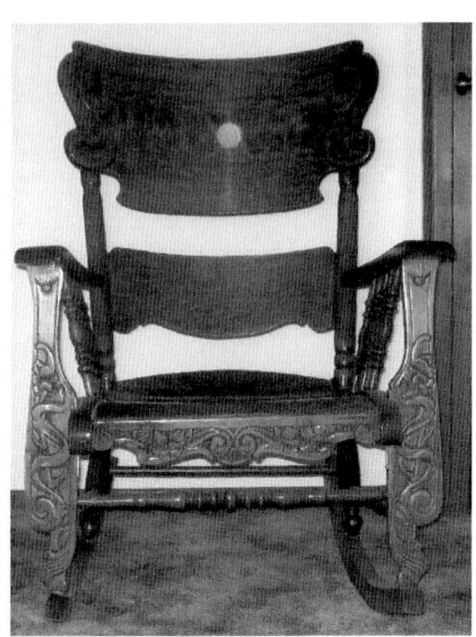

Mike Doolittle lovingly repaired this chair for his mother while he was still in high school. *Courtesy of Mike Doolittle.*

The old gentleman taught the young man about braces and turnbuckles, and Mike meticulously and expertly glued the chair back together. He took his finished project to his woodshop class at school, where he refinished it. When it was done, he gave the beautiful rocking chair to his mother. To this day, she considers it the most precious gift Mike ever gave her.

After high school, Mike graduated from Clackamas Community College and then went on to Oregon State University, where he majored in business administration with a minor in psychology. He originally planned to be "a big shot and run some large corporation," but in 1980, he recognized his true calling. On April 9, he opened Mike's Second Hand Store at Highway 224 and Main Street in Estacada.

He frequented garage and estate sales as well as surplus warehouses, bringing back loads of goods to stock the shelves. Disappointingly, these forays failed to fill the space. Then Audrey found an ad in the paper for Ralph Alsman Auction on Eighty-Second Drive in Clackamas. Mike had discovered the mother lode of castoffs and became a regular auction bidder.

The store in Estacada was soon filled to overflowing, despite the fact that customers swarmed in to carry off one or more treasures. Mike approached Don Fancher, from whom he leased the space, and arranged to use the one-hundred-foot-wide basement. With Don's OK, Mike cut a hole in the floor and built stairs to the lower level.

Mike was an exemplary merchant. One person who helped influence his business ethic was John Campanella, who had a grocery store at the crossroad of the old Eagle Creek Road and Kellendonk Road (renamed River Mill Dam Road). In front of his counter, Campanella had a barrel containing blocks of black chocolate. Some customers couldn't afford to buy treats for their children after they paid for their groceries. At the conclusion of every transaction, however, Campanella would come around the counter. With great theatrics, he would reach into his pocket and solemnly open his knife. Then he would carefully shave a sliver of chocolate off that block and hand it to any child accompanying a parent.

Customers left believing that they had gotten a deal, and the children knew they had received a gift. Mike never forgot the feelings of goodwill that small act created. It was an example of good business sense and the psychology of selling, which Mike incorporated into his own ideas of how to conduct business.

Years later, Mike saw two kinds of children in his own store: those who wanted everything and cried if they couldn't have it, and those who quietly asked their parents if they could have a particular toy. He left the demanding ones to their parents, but if a child who'd asked nicely was still refused by his parents, Mike would often walk out to the car and hand the child the toy as a gift.

Mike priced items to sell, believing that turning goods over was more profitable than putting a high price on something in hopes of a huge profit, then having the item gather dust waiting for just the right buyer. Mike's theory was to never buy something for $1 then sell it for $1,000.

Whereas many dealers tried to jack up prices in an attempt to make more with every sale, Mike figured that doubling his investment was good business. If he bought a dish for fifty cents, he priced it at a dollar. His theory of "a good price and a good deal" paid off. As a result, his clientele ranged from owners of other secondhand stores, to hoarders, to antiques dealers.

Mike's store garnered a reputation for housing the fascinating. If you wanted anything, you could probably find it there. One time, the ball on top of the city hall flagpole broke, and city manager Greg Ellis sent an employee to Mike's to find out what he might have. What the person took back to city hall was an antique brass toilet float. Unlike later ridged ones, this float was smooth and round and beautiful. It soon graced the pole atop Old Glory.

Mike's business was so successful that, two decades after opening his first store, he built a 10,500-square-foot building next door and moved in. Most secondhand dealers make regular trips to the dump with slightly damaged or slow-moving merchandise. Mike repaired what he could but never threw items away. Occasionally, he attached a "Free" sign and put items in front of the store. When it was time to move to the new store, however, he brought in a dumpster for things that hadn't sold in a while.

Mike was surprised and gratified when many citizens of Estacada came together with hands and hand trucks to help move the contents of the store to the new location. Once all the goods were in place, Mike found he had more room than he had anticipated. He went out to the dumpster and brought everything back in to fill the shelves in the new store.

Standing guard on either side of the new entrance were a huge wooden cigar-store Indian and an eight-foot, six-inch redwood statue of Sasquatch holding a sign: "Shoplifters will be eaten." Both pieces were hand-carved by Dewey Peasely, son of a famous totem pole carver. A fountain by metal artist Brent Lawrence, surrounded by a rock garden made from Mike's childhood rock collection graced the side of the building. The jingle of twenty-five bells greeted customers as they opened the front door.

Mike's Second Hand Store emerged not only as a retail store but also as a tourist attraction. Business owners brought buses full of their employees to the Estacada store. Area residents who had guests from out of town always included a trip to Mike's in their tours of outstanding landmarks. The unique store attracted repeat customers from as far away as California.

Going to Mike's was an adventure. Almost anything a person might want could be found by wandering up and down the aisles on the main floor or

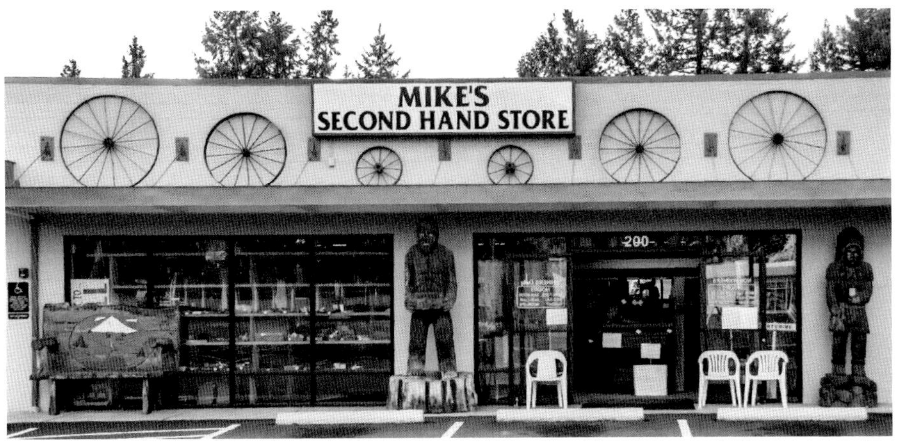

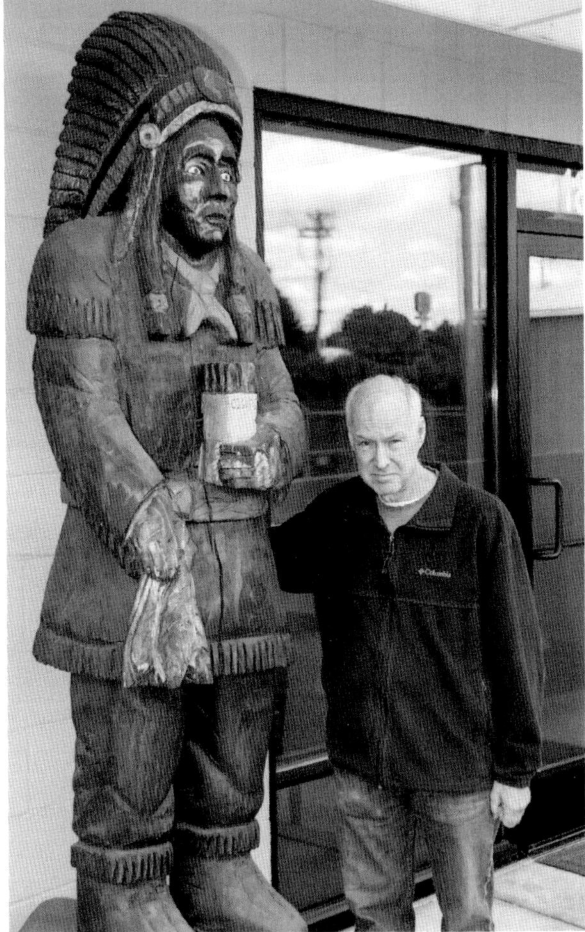

Above: Mike Doolittle's store attracted townspeople and visitors alike. They often walked away with a new treasure in their hand. *Courtesy of Mike Doolittle.*

Left: Dewey Peasely carved this cigar-store Indian, which stood in front of Mike Doolittle's secondhand store. *Courtesy of Mike Dille.*

by browsing among myriad pieces of furniture and old trunks in the spacious area downstairs.

There were shovels and silverware, knickknacks and knives, pictures and pans and eight-place dinner settings of bone china. A bedpan below a shelf holding a patchwork quilt might be filled with tiny dog statues. Customers found timeworn appliances sitting across crowded aisles from tools and kitchen gadgets that grandpa and grandma used to use. This was a veritable museum of memorabilia.

Mike was passionate about the items he sold. He knew exactly where each item was and its price. Customers were warned by signs around the store that read, "Please set things back as you found them." Another one on an antique music box said, "Don't touch this, no matter how entitled you may feel." He always said, "For some reason, I see the value in everything." Still, he was never ashamed to embrace the term "junk shop."

Mike wasn't shy about voicing opinions about himself, his business or life in general. He referred to himself as a "cranky old buzzard," claiming that he owed his longevity to hard work and a willingness to be gruff with customers. "This business draws the best and the worst from people. I've run all the jerks and thieves off," he said proudly.

Those who kept coming back were regulars who rarely failed to find one or more items they "couldn't live without." Some people came in to visit or simply to stand around and watch Mike's distinctive methods of dealing with customers or because they appreciated his outspoken, wry sense of humor.

Mike made some sacrifices in order to pursue his dream job. He single-handedly ran his store, which was open seven days a week, taking days off only for family emergencies. He visited garage and estate sales in Clackamas County, Multnomah County and beyond before opening his store at 9:00 a.m. on weekdays or noon on Sunday. During the trips, he looked for interesting items rather than "big scores." With a twinkle in his eye, he would tell customers, "I go out and hunt it down, kill it, skin it, clean it up and sell it."

On occasion, Mike found a sale so exciting that he didn't make it back to the store before the opening time painted on the door. Regular customers waited, relishing the knowledge that they would be the first to see something new and fascinating when Mike returned. One time, however, a customer became concerned that something had happened to "her" junk dealer. She went across the street to the Estacada Fire Station to ask if they knew whether he was all right. Firefighter David Long was certain that Mike was OK, but he told the woman he'd check out the town's garage sales. Sure enough, he found Mike at one of them, adding another piece to a large pile of purchases. David returned to the station, assuring the woman that the store would be open soon.

Mike had a soft spot in his heart for children and the elderly. He was filled with generosity, and he quietly shared what he had with the needs of his town. Over the years, he contributed to the Estacada Fire District fundraising raffle. The Estacada Community Center had trouble raising enough money to buy its first bus and was ready to give up until Mike stepped in and paid the $1,030 balance.

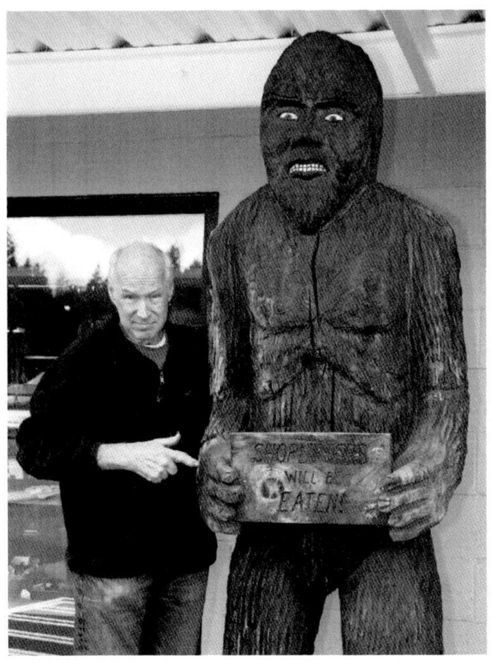

Dewey Peaseley's carving of Sasquatch warned customers that "Shoplifters will be eaten." *Courtesy of Mike Doolittle.*

When he observed that the community center parking lot was riddled with potholes, he paid for resurfacing and repaving. In his inimitable style, he commented that he "couldn't bear to see those old folks fall and break their necks."

In 1993, Estacada School District superintendent Dr. Scott Clark mentioned to Mike that, due to a lack of funding, the district was in a supply crisis. Mike responded by purchasing ten No. 2 pencils each for all students in the entire school plus ten pencils each for all home school students. He received thank-you letters from children: "Thanks for the pencils. I really needed them." "I am writing with one of the pencils you gave us." "We are running out of money—I will use these wisely." "I will use some and save some for later in the year." "I am running out of pencils, so this helps a lot. The only problem is that I have to do my homework now!"

Mike was an icon in Estacada. Residents were dismayed when, after thirty-five years as the area's favorite "junk dealer," he retired at age sixty-two. When asked why he made the decision, he said, "I've had a blast with this business, but I'm old and tired, and lately it's not as fun as it used to be." Showman to the end, Mike held a retirement sale. He placed a sign just inside the entrance: "Stop whining and start buying, folks."

For years, Mike's Second Hand Store consumed his every waking moment. Now people wondered what he would do with his time once he retired. His answer was cryptic, as always. "I'll just sit in the tavern and whine and complain about the government." Since he wasn't a drinker, that answer may not have been altogether accurate. Whatever he found to occupy his days, Mike's Second Hand Store would not be part of it.

In November 2015, the door closed on the museum of memorabilia. But oh, what memories are left!

THE GEM

No one alive today remembers the Gem Theatre that was located across the street to the east of the Estacada Hotel on Main Street.

In a *Clackamas County News* interview, Lulu Lynch, who was born in 1912, recalled going there. The theater was listed in the business directory for 1923. An ad in an early twentieth-century newspaper listed L.V. Cleworth as manager and informed readers that "Gem Theatre shows the best pictures obtainable." It also encouraged them to "Get the habit" and "Jam the Gem." This flyer invited sports enthusiasts to a wrestling match between Larry Bennett of Portland and Osupp Slovinski, "The Terrible Russian Strong Man," from Brooklyn, New York. It could have been a long match, with the "best two falls out of three or a decision at the end of two hours." The Family Theatre in the Mason Building opened in 1924. Perhaps the popularity of the new movie house led to the demise of the Gem.

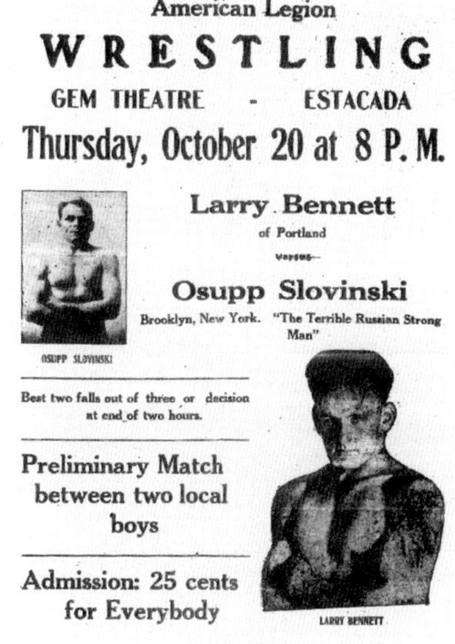

This wrestling handbill indicates that in addition to films, the Gem Theatre hosted live events. The date is unknown. *Author's collection.*

A GOOD PLACE FOR A NIGHT OUT

To get away from the stresses of life, what can beat a night at the movies? For a few hours, a person can sit in a completely dark room, shutting out everything except the enchantment on the big screen and being transported to another time, another place, another life.

For nearly sixty years, the Broadway Theater was Estacada's entertainment center. Families from Garfield, Currinsville, Eagle Creek and even Springwater, George and Viola would travel into town for relief from the monotony of rural living. Tickets cost fifteen cents for adults, but on Saturdays, the family could purchase two matinee tickets for the price of one.

The women and children would enjoy a movie while, according to lore, the men went down the street to one of the three bars to have a few and visit with the boys.

The Mason Building on Broadway was built by C.E. Stockton and dedicated on September 4, 1924. Ty and Alice Correll rented the auditorium inside the building and named it the Family Theater. Ty, a tall, slim, cigar-smoking man, accompanied the silent films on the organ below the stage, following the musical scores shipped with the film reels. When "talkies" took over in the early 1930s, Ty played the movies' theme music in the background. Eventually, films came with pre-recorded musical scores, but into the early 1940s, Ty continued to play the organ before the movie started.

Theatergoers entered the ground-floor door in the center of the building, walking past the candy and popcorn to the back where the theater was located. The carpeted hall slanted up to the theater entrance, but inside the floor slanted down so that the film was visible over each row of seats. A short set of stairs led up to the cry-room, which had a glass front. Here, mothers with babies could watch without disturbing other customers.

Up a few more steps, an all-metal room housed the two projectors. The projectionist's job began when he picked up the metal cases of film at the bus station. A movie consisted of four to six reels of thirty-five-millimeter film, each of which had to be transferred to the reels that fit the theater's projectors. Previews of upcoming films, arriving in small cans, were spliced onto the first reel.

The projectionist had to pay close attention to the film as it ran. On each reel, he marked on the film a few frames before that reel ended the letter *Q*, which stood for "cue." This alerted him to start the other projector at the proper moment so the story's continuity was not interrupted.

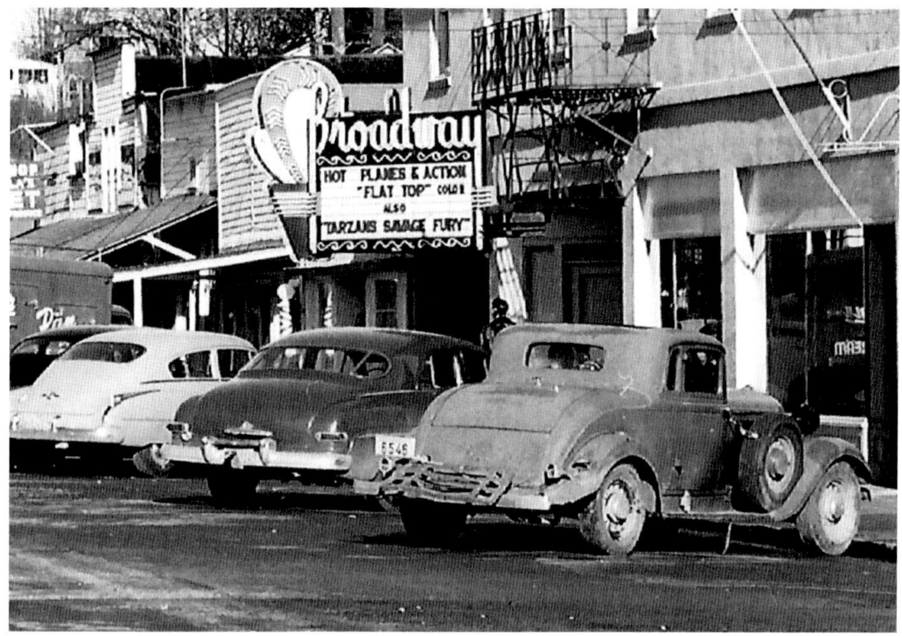

The colorful marquee of the Broadway Theatre listing the movies being shown at the time was brightly lit each night. *Author's collection.*

The electric lights at the rear of the projectors were bright carbon-arc lamps that put out enough light to project two hundred feet to the screen at the front of the auditorium. The lamps were very hot, which made the projectionist's job uncomfortable, especially in the summer months. The projectionist also had to replace the carbon rods inside the lights every twenty minutes because they did not last long at all. The wage paid to a projectionist was minimal. As late as 1966, fourteen-year-old Steve Walls was paid three dollars a night plus all the popcorn and soda he wanted. It is doubtful that Steve or his predecessor, Leroy Rich, knew how dangerous the job was.

The walls of the booth were metal as a precaution against fire. Carbon-arc lights were extremely dangerous. The excessive heat or sparks burned down many theaters. The lamps also emitted carbon monoxide, which, we can only hope, did not affect the young men's brains and, therefore, their school grades.

Another hazard for the projectionist was the boredom of repetition. Richard Hartwig laughingly complained that he saw *Blazing Saddles* twenty-three times.

The Broadway showed two movies each week: second-run (B-rated) films like *Devil on Wheels* were shown on Sunday, Monday, Tuesday and Wednesday; newer films like *Casablanca* or *Yankee Doodle Dandy* were shown on Thursday, Friday and Saturday.

During World War II, the nightly movies started with newsreels of the week's events. The gloom created by world events was offset by the upbeat offerings of *Pinocchio* and *It's a Wonderful Life.*

In the 1940s, the theater introduced the double feature, with a good movie often paired with one that was not as good. The Saturday matinee was geared toward the kids, with Gene Autry westerns and the weekly cliffhanger series with Buck Rogers.

Theater owner Bill Davis, a flamboyant fellow who fancied himself a comedian, sometimes "entertained" his theatergoers during intermission with what many described as bad jokes. Some customers laughed, while others tried not to groan out loud.

By the late 1950s, the price of a movie ticket had risen to thirty-five cents. However, local merchants gave out tickets based on the amount of money customers spent at their stores. A woman's purchases might entitle her to a "free" movie on Saturday.

Wednesday night was bingo night. Moviegoers received a paper bingo card with their ticket. The lights came up between the two films, and a volunteer (who earned a ticket for doing so) spun the wheel as the theater owner called out the numbers. The winner received two movie tickets. If, after two games, no one won, the theater put five dollars into a pot. After each week without a winner, five dollars was added to the pot. Once the jackpot reached fifty dollars, patrons on the following Wednesday played as many games as necessary until someone won. Bingo was good for the theater, because the Wednesday crowds grew larger along with the pot.

Whether an upcoming film was in color or black-and-white, its preview was always in color. It nearly told the story of the film, to the satisfaction of those who would never see the movie.

Movies as entertainment reached their peak in the 1950s, '60s and '70s. Audiences packed the Broadway to see Audie Murphy in *To Hell and Back* and Katharine Hepburn and Humphrey Bogart in *The African Queen.* Teenagers gathered to view Jeff Chandler as Cochise in *Broken Arrow.* Homemakers thrilled to *Peyton Place.* Intriguing science fiction films included *Mothra, Day of the Triffids* and *4D Man. Night of the Living Dead* scared everyone.

In 1968, the superintendent of Estacada schools made an unprecedented move. He arranged with the Broadway to show an astonishing and

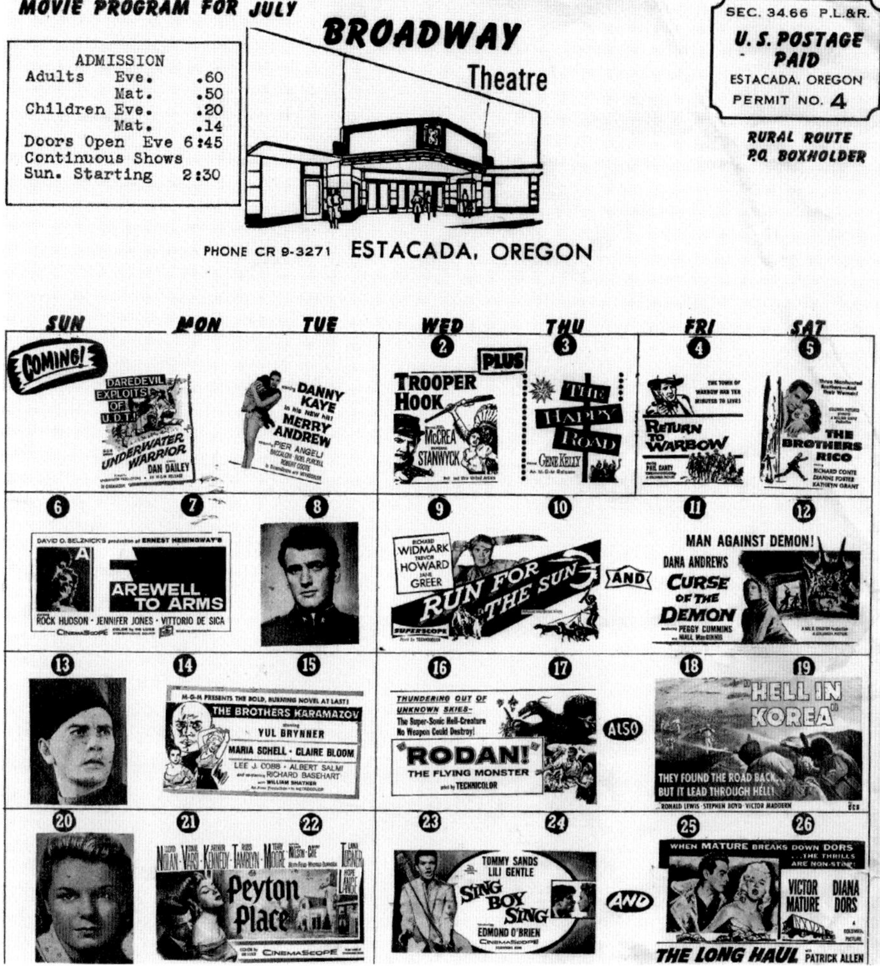

The Broadway Theatre mailed a flyer listing the movies that would be shown in the coming month to Estacada residents. *Author's collection.*

educational science fiction film during the day. Teachers escorted their classes to the theater to see *2001: A Space Odyssey*.

Run-of-the-mill pictures like *Teenage Cave Man* and *Attack of the Crab Monsters* were regular fare at the Broadway during the week. A major exception was *Star Wars*, released in 1977.

Tom Moyer's Luxury Theater chain had a contract with Twentieth Century Fox that no other theater in Portland could show *Star Wars*. Estacada was outside the Portland city limits, so Broadway owner Bill Davis ordered the movie and showed it every day of the week. His ticket price was fifty cents—less than half of that charged by Portland's theaters. For months, people flocked to see the film. Customers drove out from Portland for the viewing, until the Luxury chain threatened legal action and forced the Broadway to stop showing the film.

Davis continued to show first-run films like *Planet of the Apes*, *Benji* and anything with John Wayne, but sales began to decrease. Bill placed ads in the Estacada newspaper reminding folks that in spite of the satellite dishes being installed in the area and the fact that introduction of cable television to the area was on the horizon, "The theater is still a good place for a night out."

The auditorium needed repairs and upgrades. Bill asked Masonic Lodge 146 for a ten-year lease, which it denied. In 1985, he made the decision to close the theater.

That portion of the Mason Building became vacant. The Masons removed some of the wood seats for use in other parts of the building, where they remain. On March 15, 1995, on a dark and stormy night, as they say in the movies, clogged drainpipes backed up and overflowed, the flat roof filled with four to five feet of water, the roof collapsed and the back wall fell onto McCrae's garage, destroying that establishment. This truly marked the end of an era.

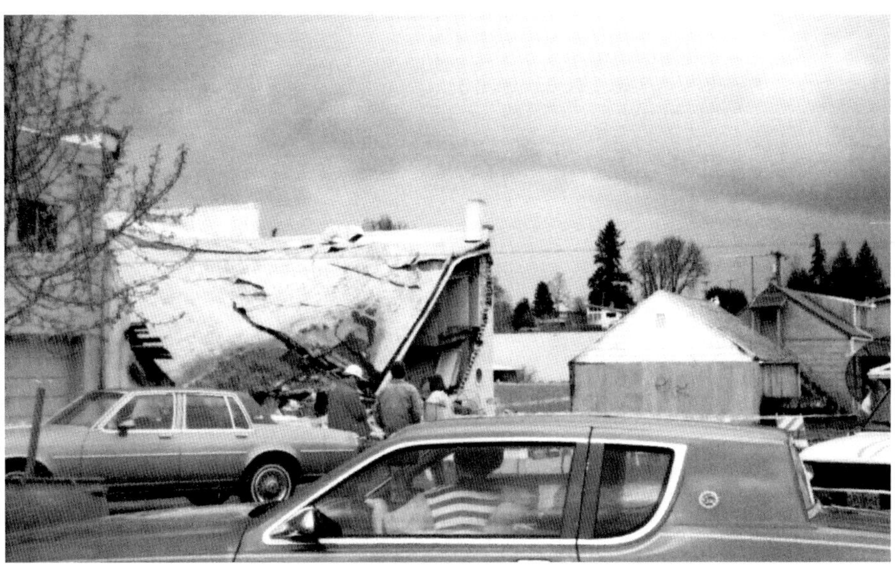

The rear of the Mason Building, showing the collapsed roof of the former Broadway Theatre. *Courtesy of Marilyn O'Grady, Mossy Rock.*

The Broadway saw five owners over its lifetime: Ty and Alice Correll, who started it; Bill and Mabel Sinclair; G.P. Rose; Gary Hart, who changed the theater's name to Broadway; and Bill Davis, who tried in vain to keep it going.

Although video rentals, satellite channels and online streaming make virtually any movie available in the home, some people say there is one thing they miss in Estacada: a theater that is a good place for a night out.

End of the Trails

When people see the name Trails Inn on the side of one of Estacada's most popular watering holes, they might assume the name denotes the "inn at the end of the trails." After all, this is a city where logging, farming and recreation trails converged.

Not so. The name comes from a surprisingly different source. The two-story brick building on the northwest corner of Broadway and Southeast Fourth Street was built as the First State Bank, which opened in June 1906. On November 21, 1923, a fire on Broadway destroyed half of the entire block on the east side of the street. The bank was severely scorched but quickly repaired.

However, the bank closed in the 1930s, and the building became a restaurant. It was later purchased by a man who moved into the rooms above the establishment. He remodeled the restaurant into a café with a bar called the Timber Room in the back. His name was Don Trails, so he renamed the building after himself: Trails Inn.

The Timber Room was popular with loggers. They gathered there before dawn in case a timber company rep came looking for fellers or buckers. And after a long day, they would relax in the booths with a beer or a shot.

But the guys didn't always stay in the Timber Room. Instead, they followed a well-worn trail south down the block into the Pine Cone Tavern. After tipping back a few there, they moved farther along the trail, east to the Sportsman's Club across Broadway. Finally, they would circle back to Trails Inn. It is a coincidence that the old bank building bearing Don's name was also the end of the trails.

Those who made the circuit more than once were, as people referred to it, "lost in the triangle."

ANOTHER KIND OF PARK

Isaac Marvin Park, born in 1860, was an early entrepreneur. Although he lived in Springwater, he chose to become proprietor of his own mercantile in Estacada in the late 1800s. The business occupied a building on the corner across the street south of the bank and next to the Pine Cone Tavern. On his ninety-fifth birthday in 1955, an article in the local newspaper regarded him as "one of the few remaining pioneers of the Estacada district."

Mr. Park and his wife, Catherine, were gentle people, well liked by their neighbors. They had one son, James. In 1910, James married a sweet girl named Maude, who gave birth to their son, Glen, in Springwater on September 11, 1911. The new parents had no idea that their boy would become well known not only in Estacada but also in many other parts of the world.

Glen, who attended Estacada Grade School, had many talents, and he was determined to use every one of them during his lifetime. He also inherited the entrepreneurial spirit from his grandfather Isaac and is best known for purchasing the Sportsman's Club, tearing it down and building the renowned Safari Club.

6

Signs of the Times

LANDMARK

For sixty-one years, a neon sign affixed to the top of a metal pole stood at the corner of Eagle Creek Road and Kellendonk Road (renamed River Mill Road). The sign proudly proclaimed one word: Campanella.

From 1945 on, everyone who lived in Estacada recognized the name as the main source of groceries for the area surrounding Currinsville. John Campanella, with his son Fred, started the market in a one-car garage with a dirt floor. Wooden orange crates stacked around the walls acted as shelves. The cash register was a fishing tackle box. The Campanellas prided themselves in offering reasonably priced vegetables, fruits and canned goods.

John Campanella served in the U.S. Army during World War I. He was stationed in Koblenz, Germany, when he met and married Theresa Hillen. While still in Germany, Theresa gave birth to a son, Joseph Walter "Wally."

Fred was born on August 1, 1929, in Chicago, Illinois. He and his older brother Wally were joined by a sister, Margaret. Tragically, when Fred was just two years old, his mother died from an infection following the birth of her third son, John Jr. Penicillin could have saved her life, but although it had been discovered in 1928 by Scottish scientist Alexander Fleming, it was not until 1942 that doctors began using the drug to treat infections.

After their mother died, the siblings stayed with various aunts and uncles in Chicago. Fred was five when his father married Alice, whom Fred described as "the epitome of the wicked stepmother."

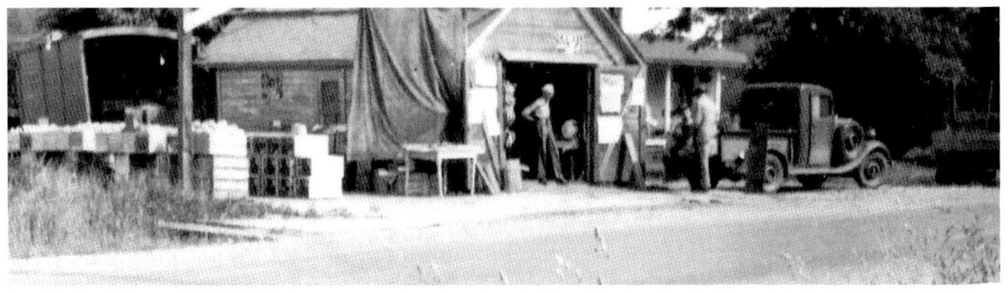

Above: John Campanella and his son Fred started their grocery store in this garage on Eagle Creek Road in 1945. *Courtesy of Fred Campanella.*

Opposite: Five-year-old Fred Campanella was a happy child until his father married, in Fred's view, a wicked witch. *Courtesy of Fred Campanella.*

Work became scarce during the Great Depression. In 1941, the Portland shipyards were hiring workers, so John Campanella brought his family to Oregon. John was happy at work, but his new wife's actions made Fred increasingly unhappy. At the age of thirteen, Fred had had enough, and he left. For some time, he stayed in his car or bunked at the homes of friends, but he eventually returned home.

Even during this tough period in his life, Fred continued to attend school. This proved to be a good decision; not only did it provide him with an education, but it also put him in a position where something wonderful happened. One day, Fred became enamored of fourteen-year-old Leona Lynch. He was playing football when the ball flew to the sideline and Leona caught it. She kicked it back, but her shoe went with it. Fred picked up the shoe and refused to give it back. Reminiscent of the story of Cinderella, Fred returned the shoe later that day. That, as they say, was the beginning of a beautiful romance.

Leona was born on December 23, 1930, in Oregon City, the daughter of Lulu Brown and Earl Lynch. Earl drove log trucks for a living. Leona had three sisters, Gladys, Sylvia and Charlotte, and one brother, George.

Fred proposed in 1947, when he was seventeen and she was sixteen. She wore her Grandmother Brown's wedding dress as they were married in the Estacada home of her father's mother, Grandmother Pinkley.

Fred's proposal included the words, "Marry me and I'll get a home for you up on Rich Man's Ridge." He was true to his word. In 1966, he bought her a home on Boulevard Way on the hill above Estacada, where they lived for their entire married life. "The only problem," Fred said, "is that then the Rich Man's Ridge moved up the hill above us."

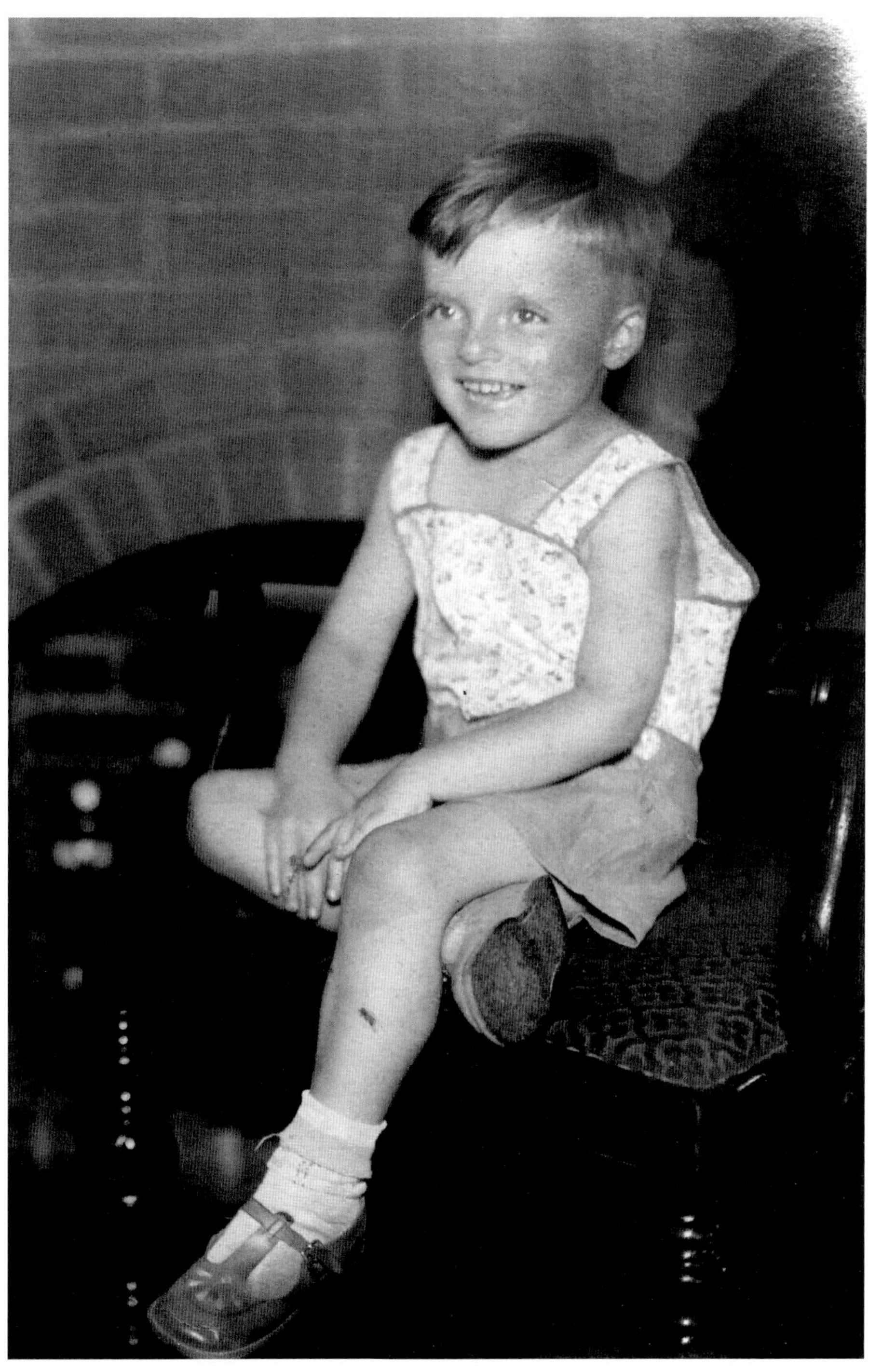

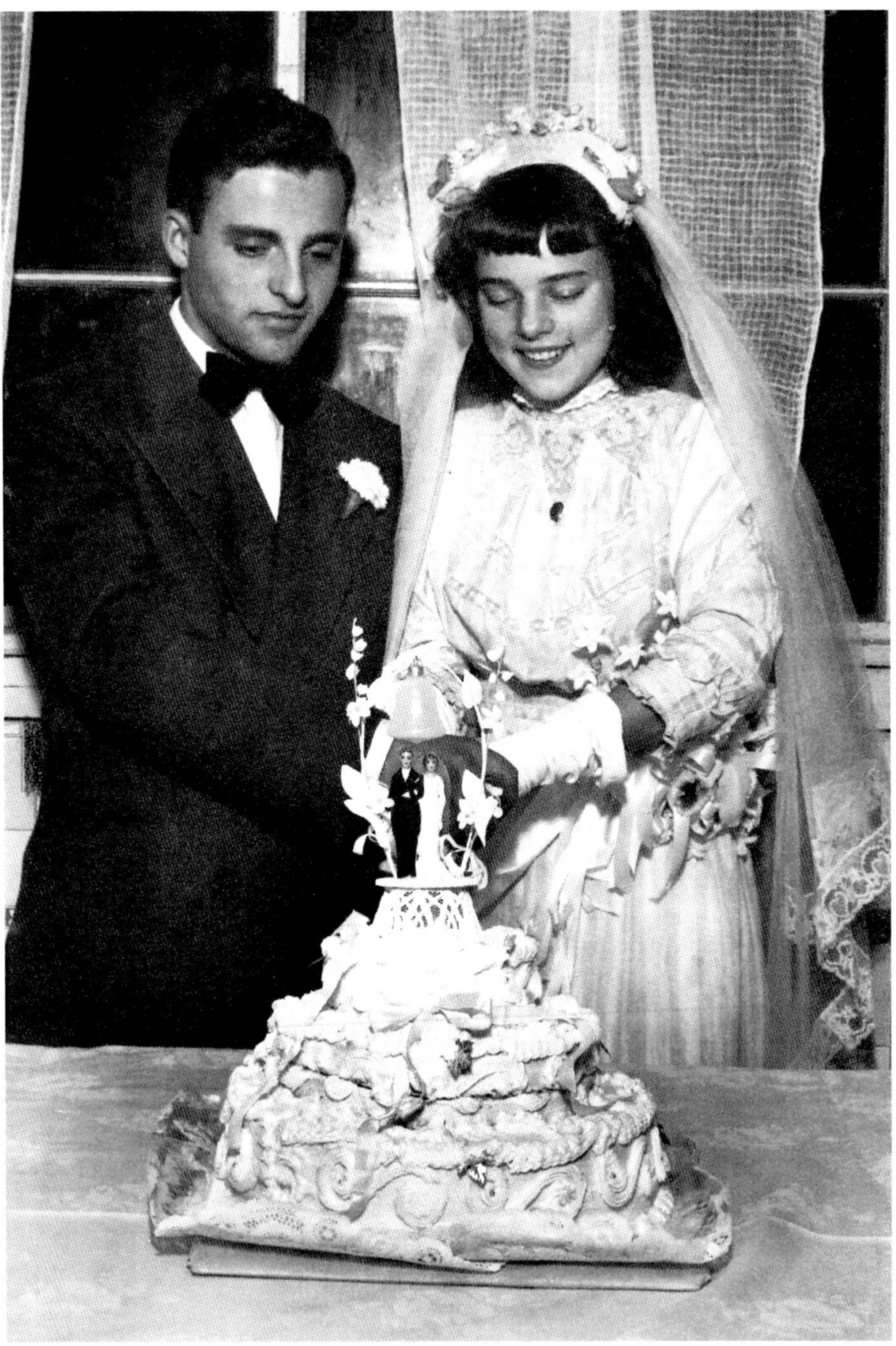

Seventeen-year-old Fred Campanella and his new wife, sixteen-year-old Leona, cut the cake at their wedding in 1947. *Courtesy of Fred Campanella.*

During their long life together, the couple had eight children, four boys and four girls, and sadly lost one son at birth. By 2016, their family had grown to include thirty grandchildren and sixty-nine great-grandkids, which made Fred exclaim, "I could have started a country."

After they were first married they moved to Seaside, where Leona's family lived. Fred started working at Safeway, and then the couple moved to Astoria, where he worked for Piggy Wiggly. He learned valuable lessons about the grocery business, which he put to good use by returning to Currinsville and joining his father at the family grocery store.

In addition to managing and working at the market, Fred ran a sixty-nine-acre farm on Eagle Creek Road, down toward Estacada from the store. At any one time, he had acres of hay, 100 head of cattle including a beautiful registered bull, a 1,500-pound boar, 125 wiener pigs and 35 butcher hogs. Fred sold the meat, which was cut and packaged by Lee Meat Company in Sandy, to individuals. Fred, who worked seven days a week, said, "The animals didn't know what day it was. They just knew they were hungry. They had to be fed."

Leona was busy taking care of the house and family and sewing clothes for the children. Quilting became her hobby. Leona recalled that, as a young child, she went to quilting meets with her grandmother Nettie Pinkley and watched her create a quilt. After her children were grown, Leona joined the renowned Skip-a-Week Quilt Club, which met at the Garfield Grange. She was president of the club for nine years and started a yearly quilt show, held during Estacada's Summer Celebration.

Business in the garage/store on Eagle Creek Road increased steadily. In addition to produce and grocery staples, it carried new products as they were introduced. As an example, the store was the first in the area to carry Swans Down Cake Mix, the very first packaged cake mix, available only in white. Like most foods of the era, it contained no preservatives.

The store continued to thrive, warranting a better building, so the Campanellas built a new store in front of the original in the garage. Once the frame was up, Fred finished the building by acting as carpenter, electrician and plumber.

The new store, with its dark, warm plank floors, was filled with wonderful smells. Customers carrying woven-wood market baskets on their arms wandered down the aisles of fruits and vegetables as they made their way to the meat market at the back of the store.

Fred was the store's butcher, cutting all the meat. Most of their customers came to the store, but Fred also delivered groceries to businesses and

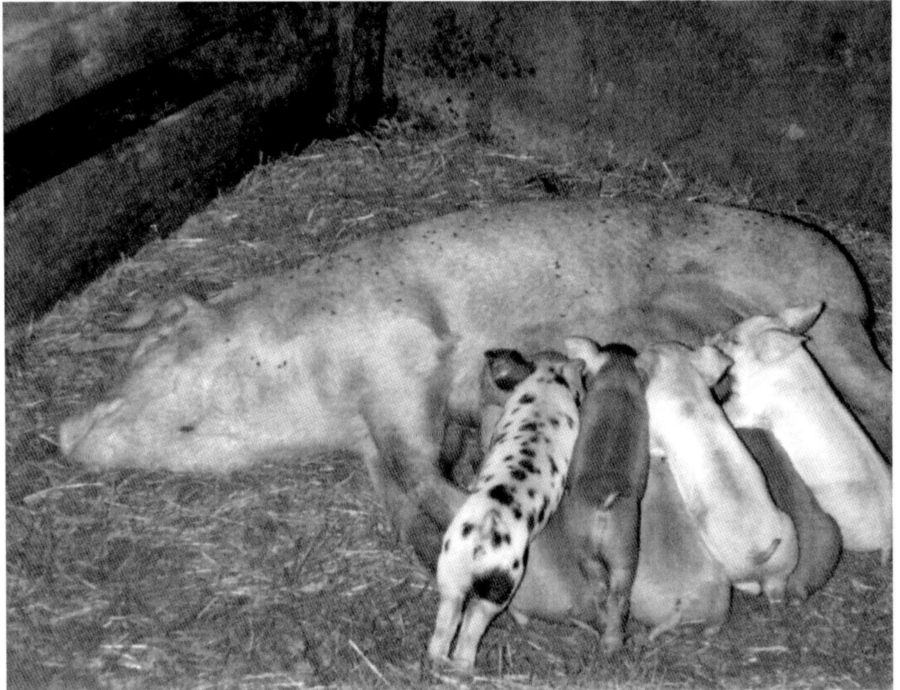

A litter of pigs, some of the many animals born on the sixty-nine-acre Campanella farm. *Courtesy of Fred Campanella.*

restaurants, such as the Safari Club and the Three Lynx School. Squaw Mountain Ranch Nudist Club wanted him to deliver supplies to them, and he agreed—"On one condition: I don't have to take my clothes off!"

In 1955, Fred responded to customers who wanted easier access to his business. He opened a second store on Broadway in downtown Estacada, which was a success over the next four years. However, the landlord refused to make necessary repairs to the building, such as fixing a leaking roof, so Fred closed the location in 1959.

Fred created a lot of excitement when he brought in fifty tons of Hermiston watermelons at a time. They were piled up so high in front of the Currinsville Market that they blocked the windows. Fred said, "A kid might steal a watermelon while I watched from the window, and I just laughed. I didn't care. At some point I had too many watermelons and I wanted to get rid of them." He originally charged a penny a pound for the melons, but finally gave them away because, as Fred put it, "People were full of watermelon."

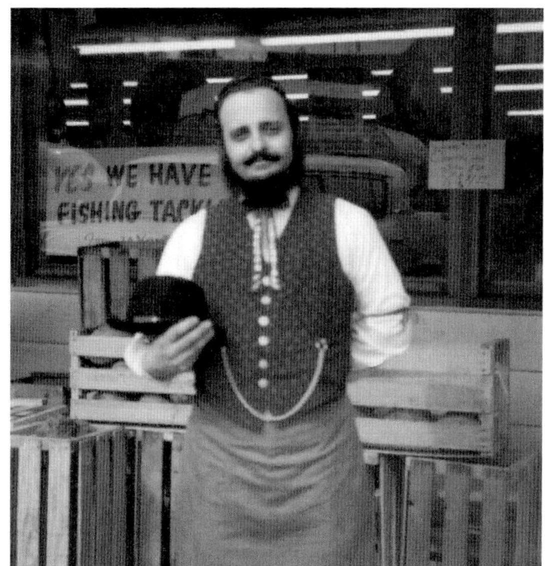

Right: Fred Campanella dressed as an 1850 store owner at his market during the centennial. *Courtesy of Fred Campanella.*

Below: The three winners of the beard-growing contest sponsored by Campanella Market during the centennial celebration. *Courtesy of Fred Campanella.*

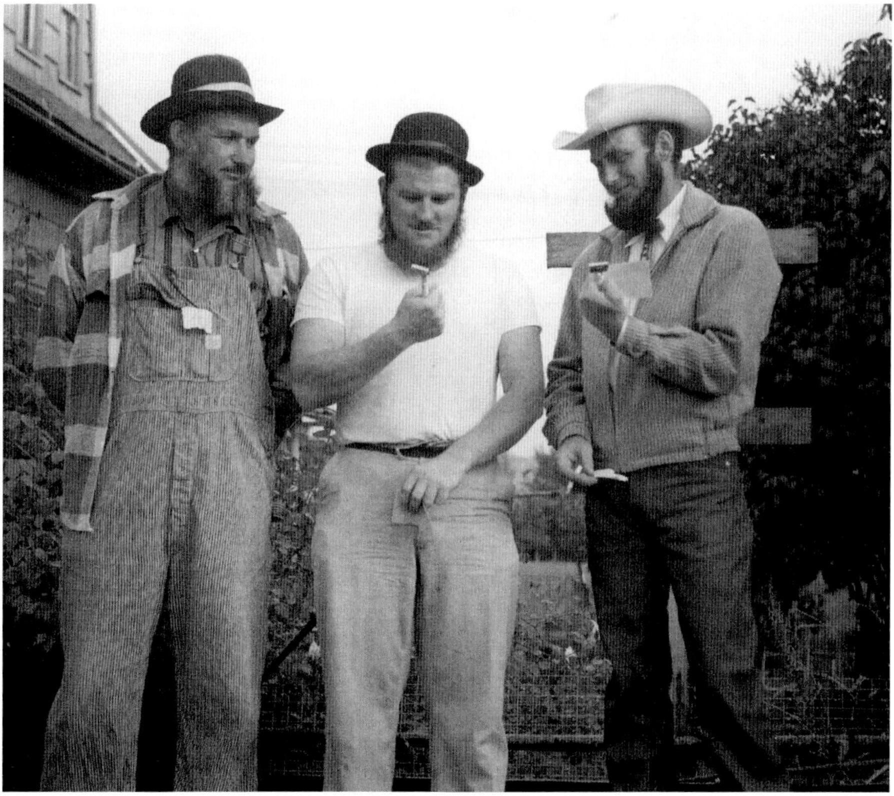

February 14, 1959, was the 100th anniversary of Oregon's statehood. For a whole year, celebrations were held all over the state, and festivities were held in many communities, including Estacada. During the summer of the Oregon centennial, Fred held an ongoing celebration at the store on the highway. One highlight was a beard-growing contest. Cash prizes were given for first-, second- and third-place winners.

One summer day, the store presented a program with historical undertones. Volunteers dressed as Indians (with costumes rented from Goodwill) and as pioneers waged a battle on the empty land across the road.

Campanella's Market also sponsored a genuine Pony Express rider. Anyone could get a specially printed envelope and buy a pre-printed commemorative stamp for one dollar. After the letter was addressed and stamped, it was placed in the rider's saddlebags. Once a week for eight weeks, Stan Adamson, the Pony Express rider, mounted his horse and carried the mail from Estacada to Salem, Oregon's capital. The letters were returned to the sender postmarked by regular U.S. Post Office mail.

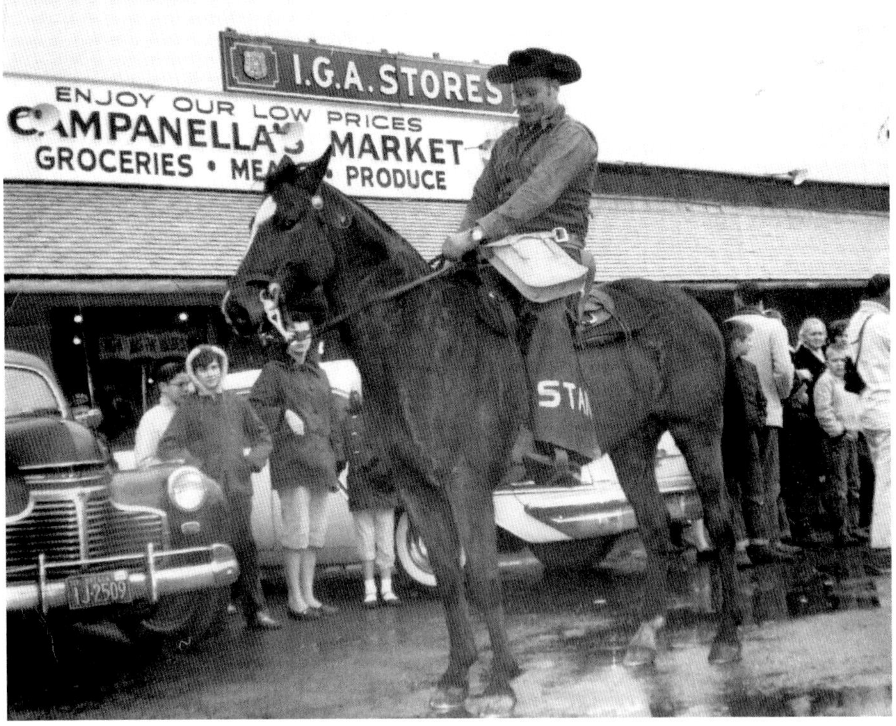

Pony Express rider Stan Adamson carried letters from Estacada-area residents to the Oregon state capitol during the centennial celebration. *Courtesy of Fred Campanella.*

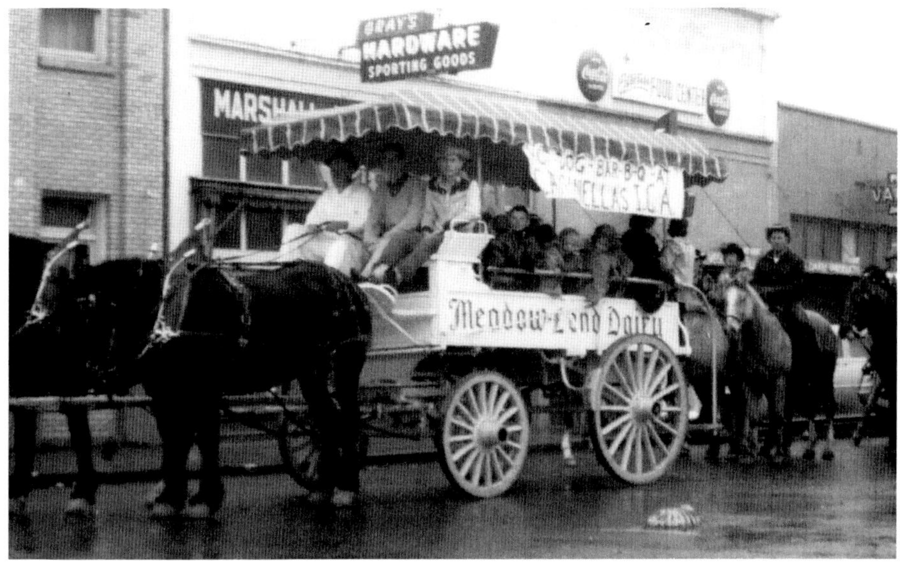

A wagon advertising a "Hot Dog Bar-B-Q" at Campanella Market was part of the rainy-day Oregon Centennial parade. *Courtesy of Fred Campanella.*

The culmination of the festivities was the Oregon Centennial Celebration Parade, replete with costumed pioneers and Indians on foot, riding horses or traveling in covered wagons, on buckboards or in the Wells Fargo coach. People lined the highway as the parade started at the store and traveled the three miles down and through the Estacada main streets and back up to the store. All of Fred and Leona's children were in the parade, wearing period clothes Leona sewed. She might have participated in the parade herself but, as she put it, "By the time I had all their costumes done, I didn't have time to do one for myself."

In 2006, Fred stopped farming and sold the land and equipment. Later, at age eighty-six, Fred said he didn't miss the store or the farm. What he always liked best was making a life for the family, which took some doing. For one thing, "They drank an awful lot of milk."

The store on Eagle Creek Road closed in 1971. The building was eventually razed, so the land stood bare. The sign remained standing. Over the years, it weathered and faded until the word imprinted on it was scarcely visible. People who passed it still recalled the store filled with economically priced goods. Moreover, they remembered the man who left his imprint on the town of Estacada. His name was Campanella.

SKIP-A-WEEK QUILT CLUB

Meeting in the Garfield Grange, a group of women continues a tradition started in 1921. The quilt club, which may be the oldest in Oregon, is dedicated to the community. It donates quilts to the Estacada Fire Department for people who have been burned out of their homes, and to charitable organizations. Despite the club's name, its members actually meet every week.

COINCIDENCE

During World War I, Estacada resident John Campanella served in the U.S. Army. He was stationed in Koblenz, Germany when he met and married the love of his life, a fraulein named Theresa Hillen. Before John returned to America with his wife, Theresa presented her husband with a baby boy, whom they named Joseph.

As soon as he was old enough, Joseph followed his father's example and enlisted in the army. He was a member of the Eighty-Seventh Infantry Division Army of Occupation, which, in the spring of 1945, was stationed in the city of Koblenz, Germany, the very same town where his parents were wed.

There, Joseph met Lil, who soon became his German sweetheart. She joyfully said "yes" when he asked her to marry him.

Joseph was one of many GIs who wanted to marry their German girls and take them back home. The army required that the American-born soldiers wait six months for a permit after applying for a marriage license. During that time, identities were verified and papers were processed. Presumably, the wait also gave the men a chance to decide if they really wanted to take the big step into matrimony.

Joseph was certain that he wanted to marry Lil, but he dreaded the six-month wait in case he was ordered to return home before they could wed. The young couple proceeded to the office on his army base to fill out the papers. The first question the clerk asked was, "Where were you born?"

"Right here in Koblenz," he said. "I was born here." Their request was rushed, and the paperwork went through.

McCrae's

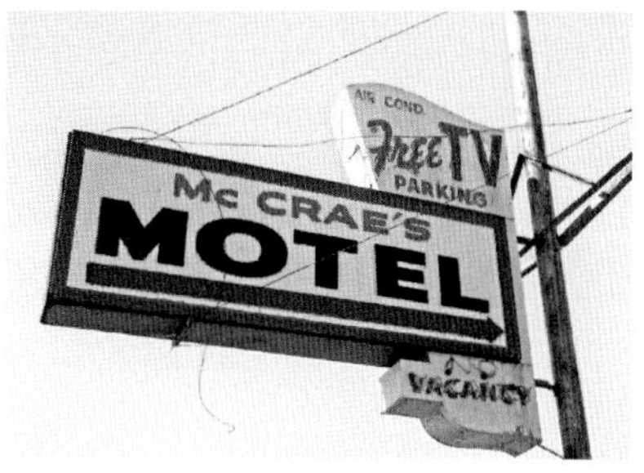

The faded sign on Main Street advertising a motel that had not operated for over twenty-five years. *Courtesy of Mike Dille.*

Thirty-two years after the last guest departed McCrae's Motel, a faded sign advertising the establishment's amenities still stands on Main Street, like a ghost of times past.

Hollyhocks, Garland McRae's favorite flower, bloom in a rainbow of colors in the alley along the entire back of the building.

A heritage rose bush joins more hollyhocks on the northeast corner of the property in a small flower garden beside the old log cabin purported to be the oldest building in Estacada.

Garland's husband, Archie, did most of the actual construction when the motel was built in the 1930s, and he painted the building a distinctive lime green. He performed all the upkeep himself, repairing electrical wiring, resolving plumbing issues and building or rebuilding anything the motel needed.

The business thrived. Since they ran the only motel in town, Garland and Archie kept busy hosting out-of-towners and men working on Portland General Electric's North Fork Dam.

But they were not too busy to take vacations. Their lucrative business afforded them the luxury of traveling to exotic locales, and the McCrae home displayed collections of hand-carved German cuckoo clocks, statues of Buddha and colorful oil paintings.

At home, Archie reveled in the thrill of riding his motorcycle. Unfortunately, he crashed the bike in an accident so serious that he was confined to a wheelchair for the last ten years of his life.

After Archie died in 1985, Garland lost interest in running the motel. She held a big sale and let go of all the rollaway beds, lamps, quilts, antiques and other motel furnishings. Once that was over, she closed herself up in her house, becoming a veritable hermit. For the next fifteen years, the motel building was unoccupied.

Mrs. McRae sold the property to Mike Misley in 2000, with a clause in the contract that she could continue living in her house for the rest of her life. However, her health deteriorated. A few years later, she was moved to a care center, where she passed away in 2003.

Going through the remnants of a deceased person's life is revealing, and the findings are sometimes odd. After he bought the property, Mike had to remove a portion of the floor in one of the former motel units. The ground underneath was littered with empty cans of Brown Derby beer, with its distinctive image of a figure dressed to the teeth, wearing a derby hat and carrying a fancy cane. It seems the men Archie hired to pour the cement foundation had quite enjoyed their work days.

Garland and Archie apparently did not believe in placing their money in financial institutions. Carl Prokop, who repaired the McCraes' television sets, said they stashed money inside the sets. He always left the paper bills in place when he replaced the cardboard backs and returned the TVs.

The dismantling of a metal shower in one of the motel units exposed a mason jar filled with silver dollars. Removal of the flour bin in the house's kitchen revealed a safe secreted behind it. The folds of sheets in the linen closet were stuffed with $100 bills.

The strangest find was in the log cabin, which had not been touched since Archie's death. The doors were padlocked, but they did not open when the padlocks were removed. Mike had to remove a small section of the building in order to get inside. He found the main room filled with over fifty 1970s-era television sets sitting on their rolling wire racks.

This final discovery was astounding. Archie had put padlocks on the inside of the doors. How did he do that and get out? The answer came when Mike located a trapdoor in the floor of a closet, which led to the crawl space under the cabin. It seems that Archie had padlocked the doors from inside and exited through the crawl space, then padlocked the doors on the outside.

McCrae's Motel is no longer. The house, cabin and rooms are now rented to longtime residents.

But, like a ghost of the past, the sign remains.

POPULATION JOKE

For many years, the Estacada population remained stable at 998. A standing joke was that every time a child was born, a fellow was leaving town.

Auto Row

The horse and wagon gradually gave way to the automobile as the preferred method of transportation—as long as the new-fangled machine could make it up a hill with a 20 percent grade through eighteen inches of mud. Everyone marveled when J.W. Reed successfully plowed through the sticky clay mix from Viola down Clear Creek to Fischer's Mill in his Studebaker Oakland Six.

As roads improved and cars gained popularity, blacksmith shops adapted, providing automobile repair in addition to shoeing horses. These businesses gradually evolved into garages that dealt exclusively with the mechanical repair of cars. In conjunction with the garages, some men started automobile dealerships. Main Street was Estacada's "auto row."

Two dealerships were built in the same location, and both burned down prior to 1930. The only one for which there is a record is the Wilcox Cascade Garage.

The exact date is not known, but the report says that fire swept through the garage, destroying its contents. Fed by oil and gasoline, the flames raced over vehicles that exploded. Mr. Wilcox, firefighters and car owners could only stand and watch. When the fire burned itself out, all that was left were the charred remains of the building and its contents. The sole exception to complete ruin was the bed and rear wheels of a 1918 truck.

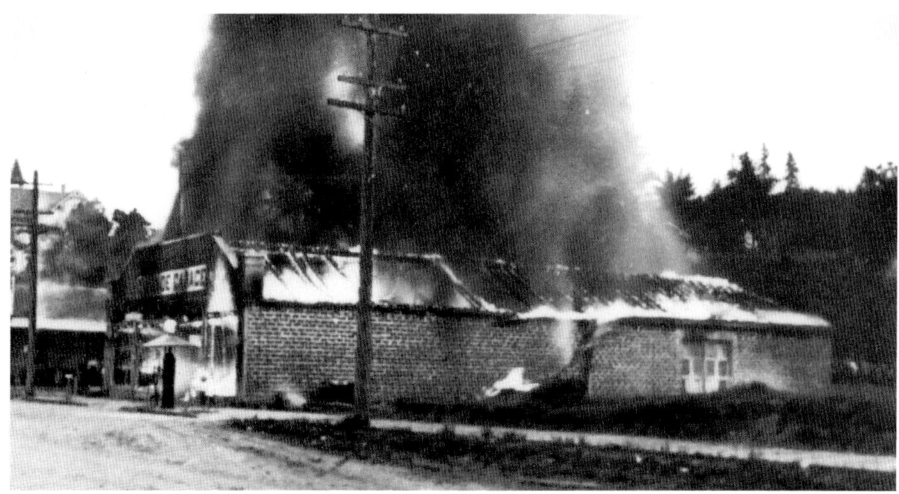

The twisted metal of the dozen or so automobile bodies were mute evidence of the once-thriving business. *Courtesy of Jackknife-Zion-Horseheaven Historical Society.*

Ray Hayden started a Chevrolet dealership with an adjoining garage on that location on Main Street in the late 1920s. Although Hayden retained ownership of the building and land, car dealers occupying the building over the years included Ray Hayden, Dick Spanhauer, George Giles, Woody Miller, Bud Husserl, the Trachl brothers, Jim Madland (a professional cowboy) and Fred McNally. McNally moved his business to the city industrial park in 1982.

The building remained uninhabited until 1988, when Hayden chose to tear it down. Estacada True Value Hardware was built in its place. It does not sell cars, but it does offer select auto supplies.

7
On the Other Side

Springwater Fire

September 19, 1902, was hot and dry. The harvests were in, and the barns were full. It promised to be a comfortable winter.

To four men who lived in Oregon City, it was a good day to put away their gear and venison after a couple of days hunting in the wilderness above Dodge. They had arranged with Jim Marrs to guide them into the forest nearly four miles above his farm. Jim had taken them into the cascades above the south fork of the Clackamas, where he knew the deer liked to cross between two watersheds.

The afternoon before, on September 18, the men had crossed a creek carrying the deer they had bagged. When they emerged from the trees, they and their clothing were wet. Despite the heat, they set a small drying fire. Come morning, they left the woods with their bounty. Live embers in the campfire awoke, caught on the dry grass and ignited a snag.

The snag was burning when the east winds came up. In an instant, the wind picked the fire up and carried it across the creek, across the land and down through Dodge. Many families in Springwater had traveled south and were away in the Willamette Valley picking hops. Smoke rose so high that it was visible in Oregon City, and the farmers who had stayed home to tend to their animals rushed to put out the blaze.

But the flames broke away and raced on. Even as people fought the fire, it became clear that the blaze was approaching Springwater. Dr. William Wallens, the local dentist, and his wife, Nellie, loaded their buggy and galloped the horses down the road, yelling, "Run for your lives!" The firestorm grew larger as it raced across the land. The flames found an easy path along the wooden rail fences, fed by the dry grass growing underneath.

All that day and night, and on into the next morning, the fire raged. It traveled northwesterly along the ridge between the Clackamas River and Clear Creek and destroyed everything in its path. The sky glowed red as blood.

As the fire roared through, Frank Millard rushed across the road to throw water on William Tucker's burning porch roof. He saved Tucker's house but, by doing so, lost his own barn. Frank disappeared, and neighbors feared he had died. In fact, he had literally passed out from the stress then crawled into a barn to rest after he came to. Nearby, Branch Tucker, owner of one of the finest farms in the county, saw everything—his home and his life's work—swept away in a few moments. The names on the list of owners of lost properties grew: Closner, Cross, Albright, Coin, Keller, Reed, Gordon, Goble, Busch, Miller, Willis, Smith and Shannon.

The conflagration traveled so quickly that people had little time to save anything but their lives. Neighbors worked through the night throwing household goods into dry wells.

Christopher and Mary Guttridge's outbuildings burned, but their house and barn were saved. Robert Guttridge's barn and granary—gone. William Lewellen's barn and crops, Mrs. Lewellen's house and contents, E.J. Brown's granary of eight hundred bushels of grain, Myers and Son Sawmill—up in flames. George Cunningham's place—a complete loss, including $200 worth of fine swine.

That east wind was terrible! The smoke was so dense that families could hardly see. As the inferno raged on, the losses mounted. Berry fields were decimated. Terrified mothers and children watched for burning limbs and branches and beat them out as they fell to the ground. Ruth Cromer's father picked her up and placed her in the buckboard with the rest of his family to take them to safety. Ruth's brand-new shoes were abandoned on the ground. Even eighty years later, she still grieved for those shoes.

The losses mounted, including Al Carey's granary, Mrs. Cherry's barn and its contents, Charles Bard's granary with two hundred bushels in grain and John Lewellen's barn. All of Al Lacey's possessions were lost, except for his granary. Howell's threshing outfit was gone. John and Mollie Stormer and their daughter Laura lost everything.

The roads were narrow, the timber was tall and dry and the fire leaped on and on. The raging fire had grown to between one to four miles wide and ten miles long. "Surely," some thought, "this must be what hell is like."

The blaze bore down on Grandpap Almon Shibley's farm. Twenty buildings, including Almon's house and barn, burned to the ground, and the hungry fire approached the field east of his son James's piece.

James's wife, Mary, carried her silver and her good china outside and buried it in the garden. She and James valiantly fought the fire. Everett and Elva, their four-year-old twins, carried little buckets of water to put out the sparks. Everett ruined his only pair of shoes stamping out the flaming cow pies. The barn, shed, water tower, blacksmith shop and house barely escaped the flames, as the nearby blackened snags bore witness. Other families were not so fortunate: the Howells, Warnocks and Kandles lost nearly everything.

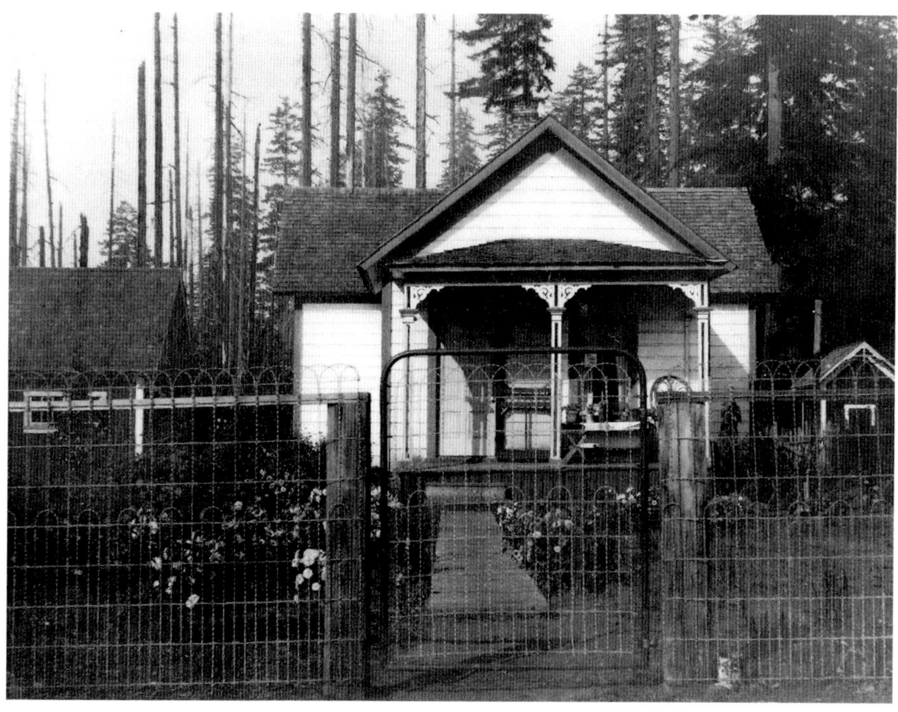

In 1920, burned snags still stood as reminders of how close the 1902 fire came to James Shibley's home. *Courtesy of Gilbert Shibley.*

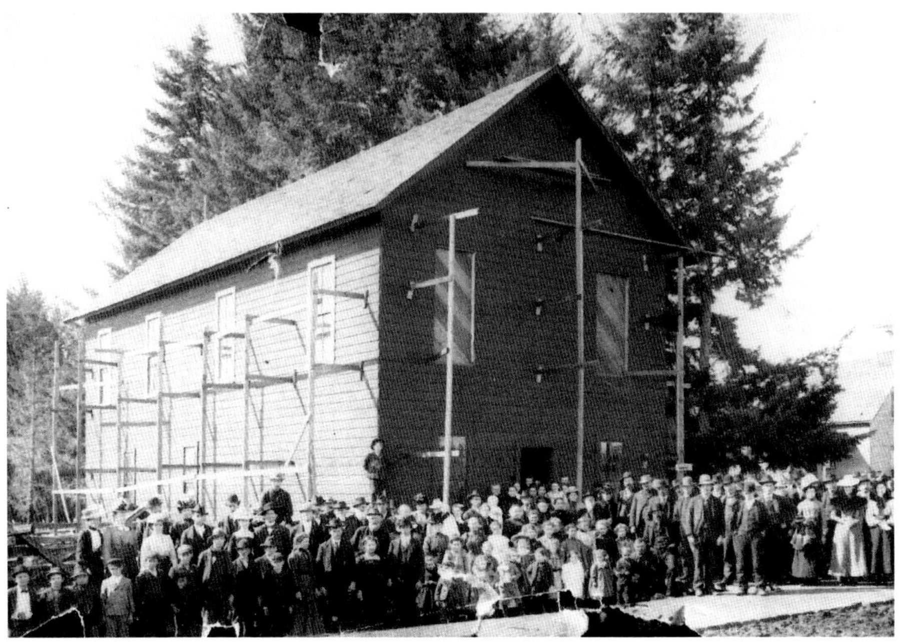

The Springwater Grange Hall was one of the few buildings that did not burn in the 1902 fire. *Courtesy of Wilma Guttridge.*

The fire reached the edge of Clear Creek Canyon near Wallens Road, and the wind carried it along the top of the canyon. Flames licked their way another three miles along the ridge to the Jubb place where, miraculously, late on Friday, the wind died down and the fire breathed its last. That night, the Shibley twins were put to bed on a blanket in the middle of the barnyard. Their pet pig crawled in beside them.

As residents returned home, they took stock of the unbelievable losses. Sixty people were homeless and destitute. Timber, cordwood and fences were decimated. Cattle burned, their carcasses strewn everywhere. Thousands of tons of hay and great quantities of grain were destroyed. Several county bridges were swept away. An entry in a resident's diary read, "So complete was the work of the flames that scarcely any grain stubble remained for stock to feed upon."

Incredibly, the grange hall survived, as did the church's manse and the store. But across the road, the church had not made it through the firestorm. Although everyone felt bad that it had burned, they had been so consumed with saving their farms that the church had not even entered their minds.

After the blaze was defeated, what was left of the town besides the few buildings and a community of brave souls? Years later, Everett Shibley said, "It was the pits for the outhouses…and a lot of open areas for new pasture."

The Name Is Hayden

In 1877, Civil War veteran James Morton Hayden and his brother-in-law William T. Smith brought their families from Missouri to settle in Springwater. James and his wife, Elsie Wooster Hayden, were proud parents of sons Charles and Howard and daughters Minnie and Emma. James and William rented a house together and worked for farmers, accepting flour, bacon and potatoes for pay. Around 1878, James's parents, Joe and Sarah Hayden, arrived from Missouri, settling in Viola.

Springwater Road overlooked the rolling hills and huge barn of the Troxel family farm. The Troxel Cutoff, a single-lane, relatively straight road, led from the farm down the hill to Estacada Road. At some point, the cutoff was extended from Springwater Road to the bottom of the hill, where cars turned left onto Estacada Road and on into town. The Troxel Cutoff bypassed the switchbacked curves of the upper Estacada Road altogether.

In the 1970s, Clackamas County renamed many roads to honor original pioneers who had lived on them. Troxel Cutoff was changed to honor pioneer settler James Morton Hayden, who had lived near the road beginning in 1877. Today, the road bearing the name Hayden runs up the hill from Highway 211 to Springwater Road.

Young Love

In the 1800s, most young people who completed the eighth grade were through with their formal education. Boys began working full time on the family farm. Girls stayed at home to help their mothers raise the younger children, learning everything they would need to know when they were married, which would most likely be soon.

Anyone who graduated from the eighth grade could qualify as teachers if they were interested in education and found a school that was willing to hire them. William Harrison Dobyns chose to become a teacher. Around

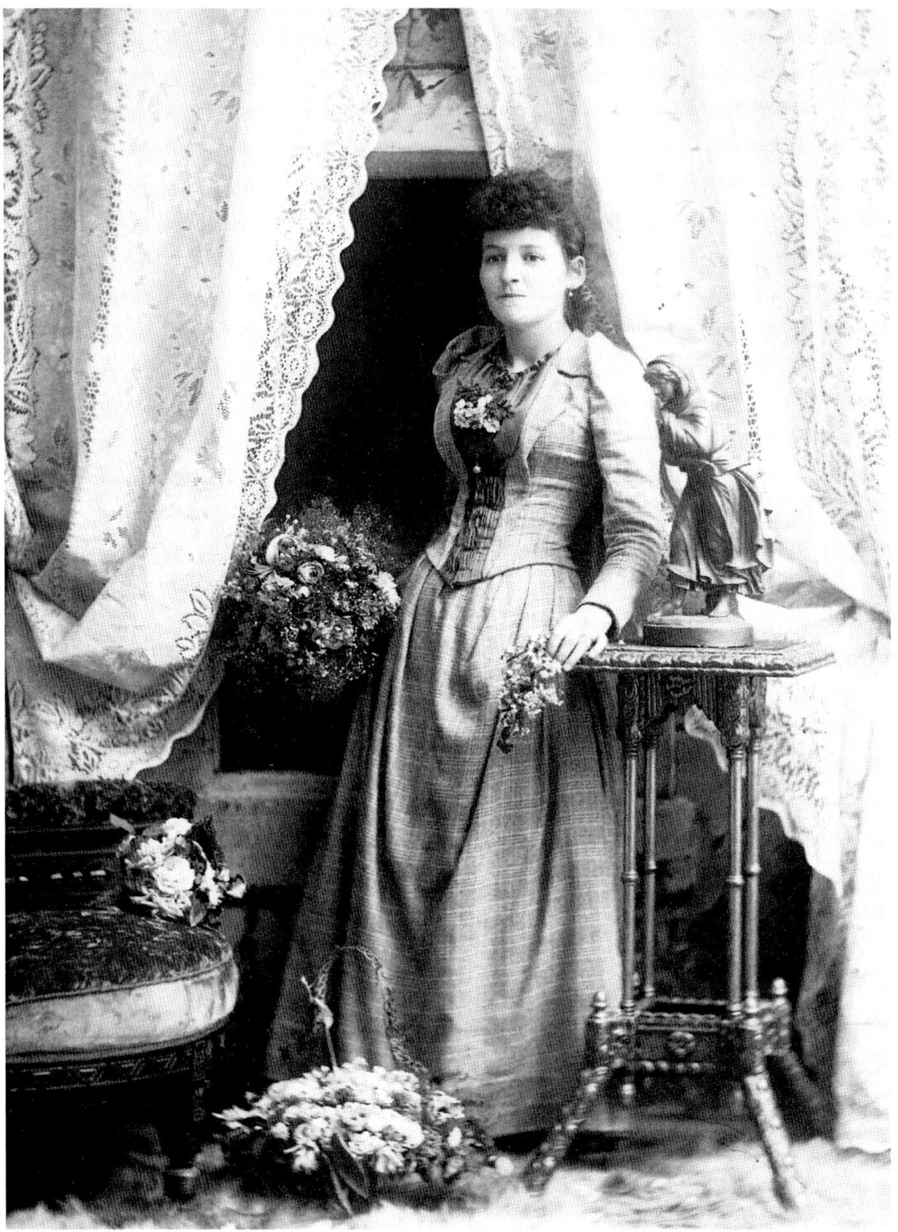

As was the custom, Emma Hayden's portrait showed her wearing a dress from her trousseau rather than her wedding gown. *Courtesy of Dottie Genereaux.*

1888, William moved from Portland when he was hired to teach at the school in Viola.

It was during a visit to her grandparents' house that Emma Hayden met a handsome schoolteacher named William Dobyns. Several years passed before William courted Emma and eventually asked James for his daughter's hand in marriage. They were wed on Sunday, December 24, 1893.

STASHED

The first roads started as horse trails and were nothing but dirt. As wagons rumbled along, their wood wheels created ruts. At best, dirt roads were bumpy in good weather. They became impassable in winter, and wagons would be mired in mud over the hubcaps.

Logging operations and sawmills began planking roads with wood in order to get logs and lumber out during wet weather. This planking practice was also a solution to traversing the muddy roads in towns and to outlying farms.

In 1907, Tucker Road outside Springwater was one of the first to be planked. William W. Tucker's daughter Violet walked the road daily on her way to school. She, like little girls of the era, wore a dress to school.

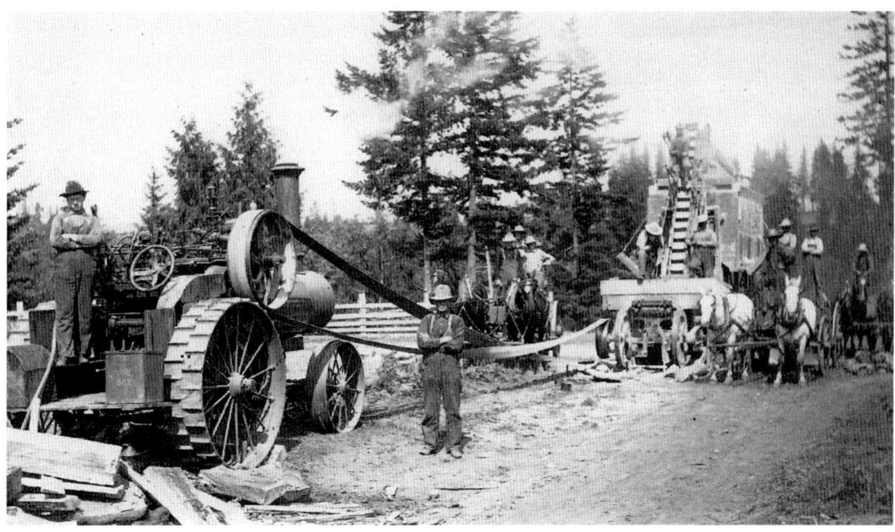

Gravel to replace the plank roads that farmers had used was made possible by the use of a rock crusher. *Courtesy of Nancy Tedrow.*

During cold weather, her mother, Laura, made sure she also wore warm woolen underwear.

Violet thought the underwear deplorable, thick and quite unattractive. On some days, she stopped on her way down the road to remove it and stuff it under the edge of the plank road where it would not be seen. She was not alone. Her siblings also removed pieces of clothing they did not want to wear and shoved those under the edge of the road.

In the early 1920s, gravel roads became popular, and Mr. Tucker removed the planks to make way for the rock crusher. In so doing, he found children's jackets, shirts and many pieces of Violet's long underwear.

8

The Good Earth

Hop to It

A reasonable source of income for people in Eagle Creek, beginning in the early 1900s and extending through the 1920s, was picking hops. There were four hop yards located on the flats between Currinsville and Barton: Trullinger and Glover each owned one, and two were owned by the Anderson family.

Hops were light and weighed by the basket. In 1910, pickers earned a penny a pound, which encouraged some young boys to drop a couple of handfuls of dirt into the baskets in an attempt to raise their wage.

Prior to World War I, Nancy Ferrel brought her sons Hugh and Bill and daughters Grace, Edith and Maude with her to Glover's, paying them each two bits a day to help her pick hops. The older children picked higher on the vines, while the younger children picked the hops that were lower or on the ground. The boys had the extra assignment of picking leaves and stems out of the baskets.

Mornings were miserable, cold and damp. By afternoon, the young ones were tired and begged to quit. Nancy urged them on, and so they kept working to please their mother…and for the twenty-five cents.

Workers pulled or pushed bins filled with hops up a ramp to the upper level of the Glover or Anderson barns. where the driers were located. Once the hops were dried, they were transported to the Blitz-Weinhard Brewery

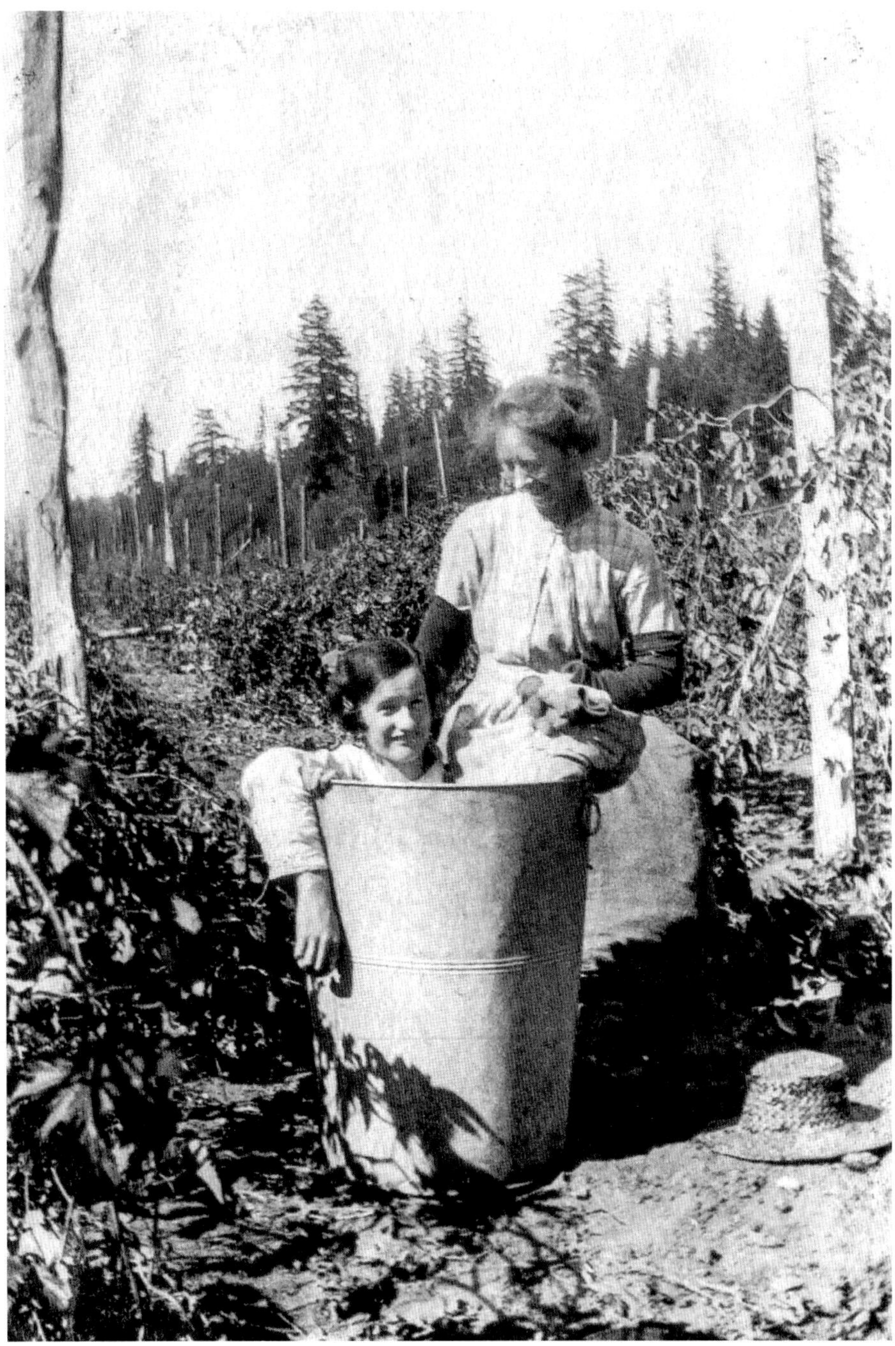

Picking hops for Mr. Glover was a regular summer job for Grace Ferrel and her aunt Rosa Looney. September 11, 1924. *Courtesy of Ruth Lazott.*

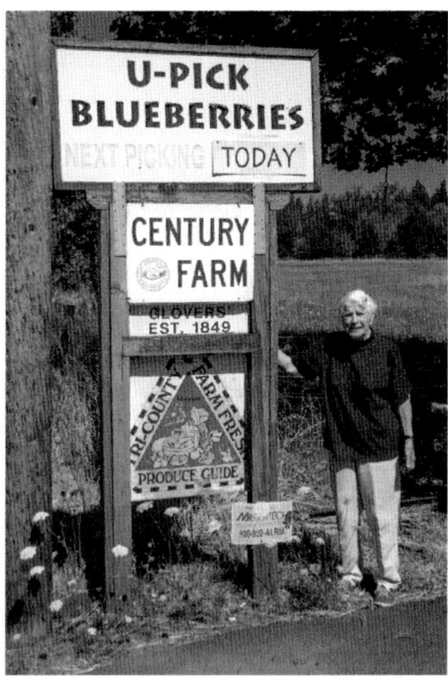

Marion Glover's family started with hops and moved to milk cows, beef cattle and then blueberries on the Eagle Creek farm. *Courtesy of Mike Dille.*

in Portland. Old-timers recalled that the workmen occasionally fell off the ramp, perhaps because they had sampled the finished product ahead of time.

To Your Health

The ginseng plant has been prized for centuries. Commonly prepared as a tea, the herb is considered a harmony remedy or longevity tonic. It has long been reputed to combat stress, improve health and well-being and upgrade athletic performance by enhancing stamina and energy. The root is most often available in dried form, either whole or sliced.

China and Korea were the largest users and producers of ginseng, until the early 1900s, when demand outstripped the available wild supply. Along with these two countries, farmers in the United States began commercial cultivation of ginseng.

John Osborne, who lived in Estacada, was one of the Americans who planted ginseng. Under the name Goldenseal Gardens, his fields stretched all the away from the Estacada High School athletic fields to the top of Regan Hill. In addition to selling the roots to China, he and the other farmers marketed them in America for use in brewing herbal tea.

Then John had what he thought was a good idea. He bottled ginseng as a soft drink so that its beneficial qualities would be easy for health-conscious people to add to their diets. To his disappointment, the innovative product failed to produce enough sales. After a short time, it was discontinued.

Houses occupy the former Osborne fields. In 2010, nearly eighty thousand tons of ginseng were produced in four countries: China, South Korea, Canada and the United States. It is sold in over thirty-five countries, with sales exceeding $2.1 billion in 2013. In addition to the root and packaged herbal teas, ginseng is now found in popular bottled energy drinks. It seems that John Osborne was just eighty years ahead of his time.

THANK THE ITALIANS

By the early 1900s, before World War I, Estacada-area farmers raised a variety of fruits, including apples, cherries and pears. However, Italian plums became one of the chief crops in the big farming communities of both Springwater and Garfield.

The Italian plum has a deep purple skin, sweet flavor and a pit that is easily removed from the flesh. This multipurpose fruit contains a high concentration of fermentable sugars, which makes it an ideal candidate to create prunes. It is easily grown in the Pacific Northwest's climate.

Christopher H. Guttridge, born in Birmingham, England, bought his farm in Springwater in 1874, where he planted 20 acres of the fruit. Valentine Lingelbach emigrated from Bürstadt, Germany, and homesteaded his 160 acres in Garfield in 1881, where he planted 70 acres of Italian plum trees. William Woodson Tucker, whose father traveled by wagon and oxen across the plains to Springwater in 1852, planted 20 acres of the trees near Springwater. Other ranchers followed their lead, and the *Estacada Progress* reported in November 1918 that 349 tons of prunes valued at $60,000 were raised near Estacada.

The harvested fruit was dried in barn-like prune dehydrators. Fires burned twenty-four hours a day for thirty-five to forty days at temperatures between 165 and 175 degrees to dry the fruit. Farmers had to cut forty cords

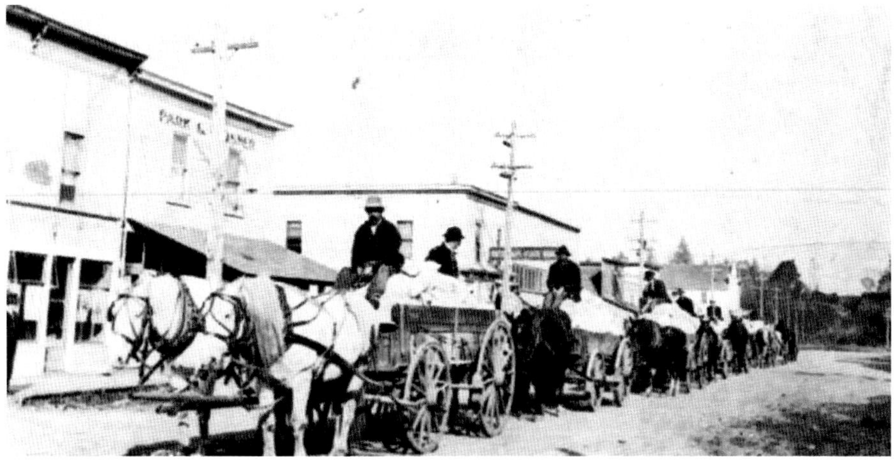

Garfield ranchers line up to load their crop of dried prunes onto freight cars for shipment to Portland. *Courtesy of Jackknife-Zion-Horseheaven Historical Society.*

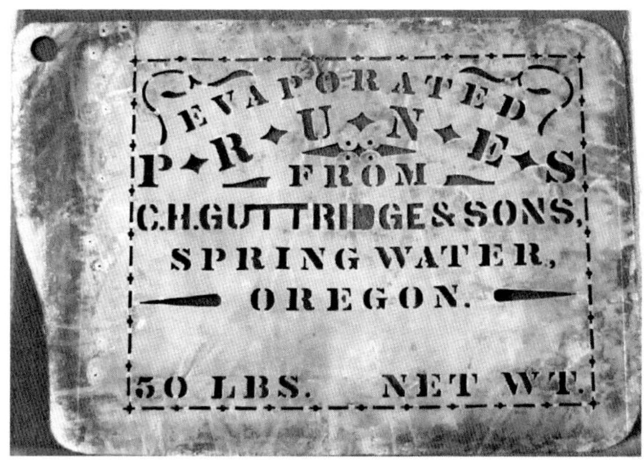

Prune farmers used stencils to mark their boxes for shipment. The one shown here belonged to Charles Guttridge. *Courtesy of Wilma Guttridge.*

of wood to burn for the heat, and it took two full-time men to keep the dryer going night and day. One load of prunes took forty-eight to seventy-two hours to dry completely.

Prior to drying, the plums were washed and sorted. The fruit was spread out on screens made of hardware cloth attached to a wood frame that measured approximately twenty-four by forty inches. The screens were placed in multilayered racks set on tracks inside a large wood tube that ran the full length of the building, gradually descending from the top of the barn to the floor. A fan run by a tractor pushed the heat from a wood furnace on the floor of the barn into the tube. As racks with freshly filled screens were pushed into the top of the tube, racks of dried prunes were removed at the bottom

Ten Springwater families owned prune dehydrators: Gilbright, Howell, Tucker, Guttridge, Smith, Lacey, McCauley, Kilgore, Closner and Schmidt. During harvest, they had fourteen prune driers going at one time, while Garfield had twelve. Garfield prune ranchers were Non Tracy, George Crawford, Charles Duncan, Henry Trapp, Lou Palmateer, Hass Tracy, Walt Snuffin, Richard Davis, Frank Thomas and Valentine Linglebach. Farmers who did not own a dryer took their harvest to a fellow farmer's barn for processing.

Once dried, the prunes were sorted for size and quality and put into boxes or twenty-five-pound burlap bags. The name of the farmer who produced that load of prunes was stenciled on each container. Those containers were loaded into wagons and taken to the freight depot in Estacada and then into railroad cars for transport to Portland, where they were sold. In addition to the large shipments, the Lingelbachs bagged small amounts of prunes to sell to local markets or to customers who came to the farm.

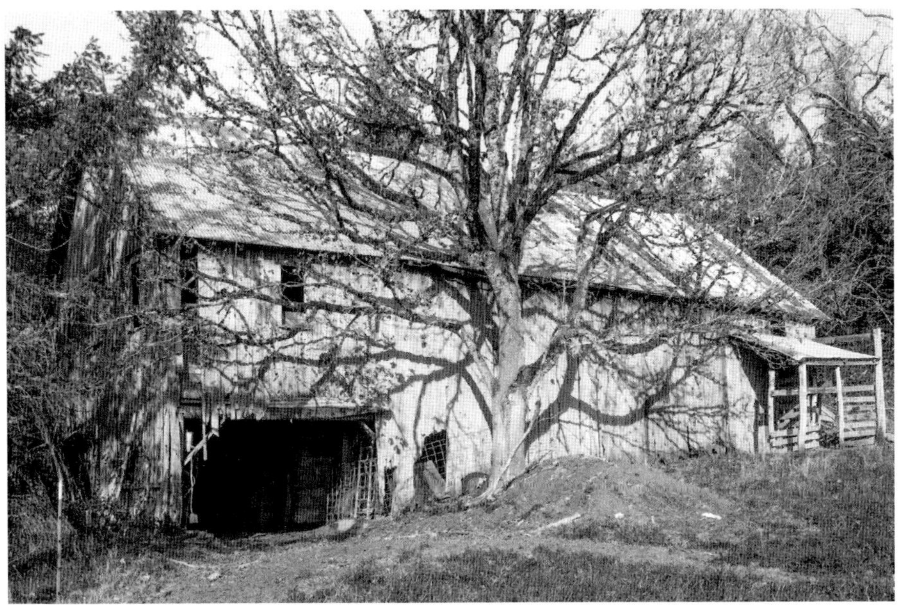

This barn is a relic of the once-active dehydrator Valentine Linglebach built to dry the large prune harvests. *Courtesy of Mike Dille.*

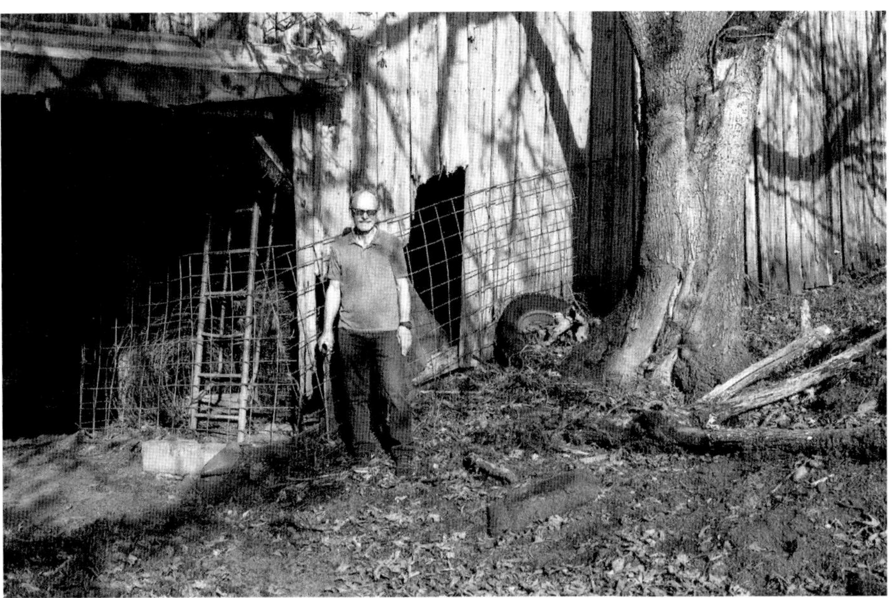

Valentine's grandson Phillip Linglebach stands by what was the entrance to the busy prune dryer his family built. *Courtesy of Mike Dille.*

In 1921, Oregon governor Ben W. Olcott declared one week in January to be "Prune Week." The *Oregonian* of February 18, 1924, reported, "The fame of the Oregon prune is becoming known the world over." Oregon's produce was being shipped as far away as India.

Production reached its height during World War II. Prices for Italian prunes skyrocketed. Long a convenient home remedy for constipation, canned prunes were in high demand by the U.S. military due to their high iron content. The army purchased and shipped thousands of cases to soldiers serving overseas. Fresh harvests from Springwater and Garfield were placed in boxes and taken by truck to a co-op cannery in Gresham. Bill Tucker recalled selling his prunes for $118 a ton.

A few relics of the prune dehydrator barns are still standing in the area, but they are gradually disintegrating. Italian prunes were good to the farmers while the market lasted. In an article about prunes in the November 1918 issue of the *Estacada Progress* newspaper, the writer observed, "No wonder our ranchers are prosperous and can afford cars."

FLOWERING

"I will daily pause to contemplate the miracles I help create in gardening" was the resolution of the Estacada Garden Club when it was organized in 1927.

Thirty women came together to share their interest in flowers. Their club welcomed everyone from beginners to masters. One of their goals was beautifying Estacada.

From the first, the emphasis was on flowers, and the ladies met to learn about plants that lent themselves to cut-flower arrangements, such as iris and dahlias. They held contests for the best zinnia garden. They went on field trips to one another's gardens or to a nursery specializing in peonies, for example. At club meetings, the ladies planned events and hosted guest speakers who talked about everything from camellias to compost.

Each year, the members sponsored a spring tea. In 1948, the club held a dahlia show and silver tea at Estacada City Hall. The highlight of each year was a two-day garden show with stunning exhibits of flowers grown and arranged by the exhibitor. Awards were given in a dozen or more categories. In 1947, the annual show featured nosegays, dish gardens, arrangements of flowering shrubs, primroses and yellow flowers. With so much interest, and so many exhibitors, the show was held in the grade school auditorium. One year, the show included arrangements of marigolds, baskets and arrangements of flowers, seeds and fruits of the same color. Another year featured exhibits of wildflowers and yard plants.

The club grew smaller over the years as more women joined the workforce and were unable to attend the afternoon meetings. The club still held garden shows at the Legion Hall or in the Estacada Senior Center, but for a variety of reasons, the show was eventually discontinued.

A strong interest in plants remains, and members continue to be active. As our world changes, the emphasis is less on flowers and more on growing vegetables. Club members have an increased interest in learning about vegetable gardening, flowers and trees, raised beds, garden pests, weeds and pruning.

For years, the club has provided hanging baskets of flowers at the entrance to the Estacada Public Library, and the flower gardens planted by members of the Estacada Garden Club continue to brighten the streets of the city.

LOAVES AND FISHES

Times were difficult in the years during and immediately following World War II. Foods that provided protein were either too scarce or too expensive for many to afford. The Catholic priest, Father Bill, found an unorthodox method of providing fish for his parishioners.

The good father took the fish (out of season) at Eagle Fern Falls. The method he used was referred to as the "Dupont Spinner." Following the precise directions he had received, he placed a stick of dynamite inside a Mason glass jar, lit the wick, closed the lid and threw the jar into the pool below the falls. When the dynamite exploded, Father Bill ran downstream to pick up the dead salmon and steelhead to take back to his flock.

When he heard the noise, the game warden came running. However, when he arrived at the scene, he deliberately and obviously turned his gaze away from the creek.

If anyone else had attempted to use this method, the warden would have immediately detained the perpetrator and levied a healthy fine on the man.

9
Wood Works

LaDee

LaDee Ridge, named after LaDee Logging Company, was up a steep rise from the Clackamas River within the Mount Hood National Forest east of Estacada. Timber was plentiful in the 1920s, but transportation of cut logs created a difficulty.

A railroad incline was built by the ridge's previous owner, Porter-Carstens Logging Company, to expedite log transportation. To bring the logs out, two sets of rails were laid side by side against the mountainside. Cars were lowered from LaDee Ridge to the North Fork River, nine hundred feet below.

In 1925, the Willamette Iron and Steel Works of Portland, Oregon, manufactured the lowering donkey that was responsible for the success of the operation. The lowering donkey was mounted on a concrete foundation at the top of the incline, 250 feet behind the headworks, which was a 26-foot-tall wood tower with sheaves mounted on the top through which the cables passed. The lift in the cables provided by the headworks ensured that they would not be caught in the load as it descended the incline.

This was a double-track counterweight design incline. The lowering donkey engine spooled out enough one-and-a-half-inch wire rope on a six-foot-diameter gypsy drum to haul cars and equipment from the bottom of the incline to the top. The line slid to the middle of the concave drum, on which water poured so it did not get too hot.

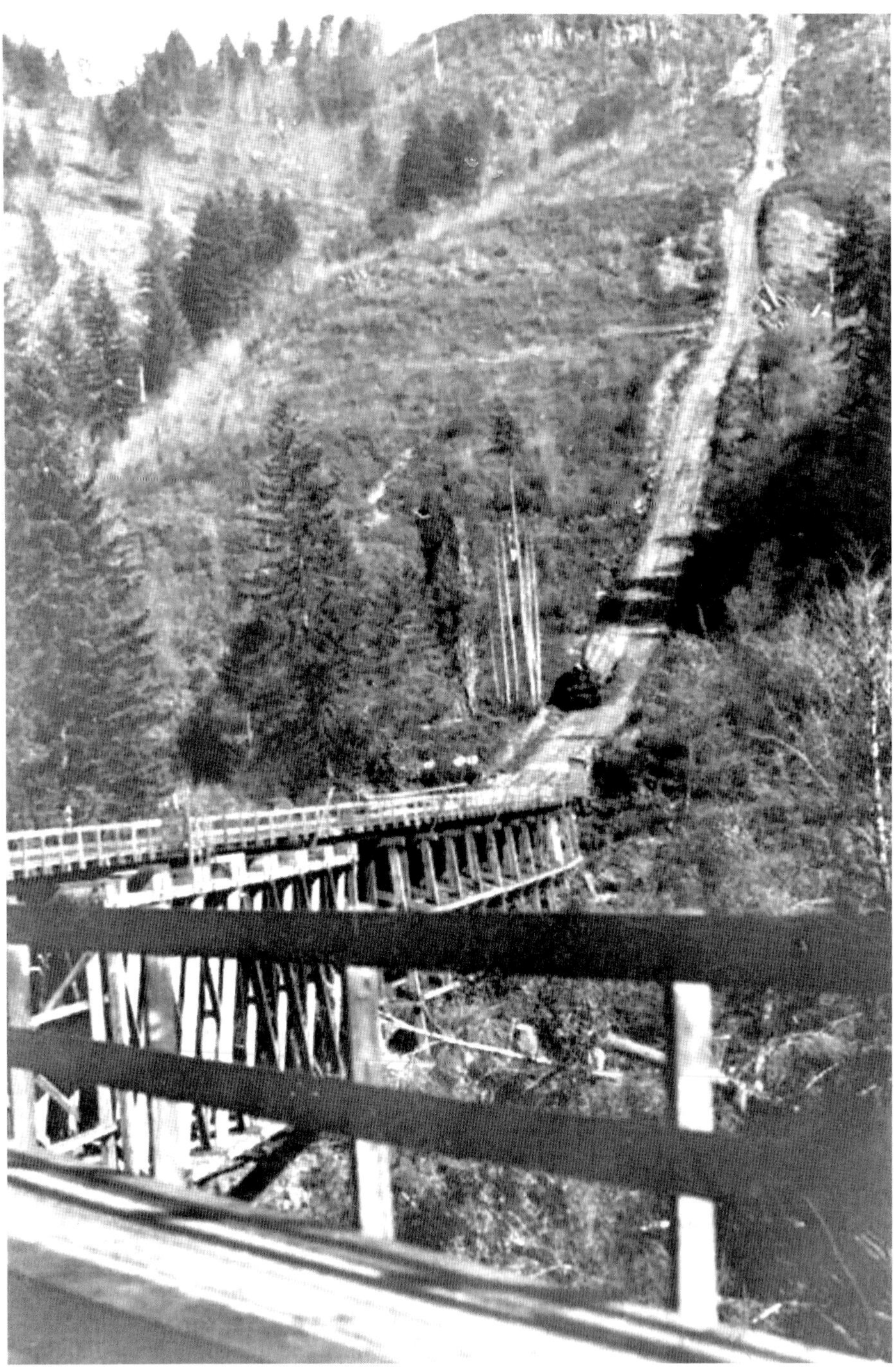

This is a partial view of the 2,800-foot-long incline that started at LaDee and ended at the Clackamas River. *Courtesy of Joanne Jaggers.*

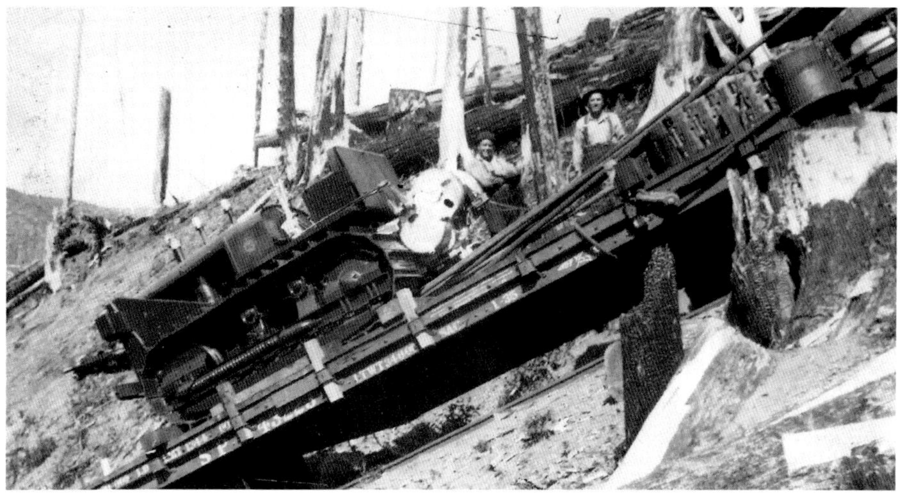

A donkey engine sat at the top of the grade, which averaged 45 percent. *Author's collection.*

Cables were attached to one flatbed sitting on the bottom and to another at the top of the incline. A cable passed through the winch at the top. As one log-loaded car went down, its weight pulled up empty log cars, as well as tank cars full of water and oil and disconnected trucks used to haul logs. The closest water supply for Camp no. 1, which was built in the summer of 1923, was the North Fork River below.

The incline was 2,800 feet on a grade that averaged 45 percent. A load of logs made the trip down the incline in three and a half minutes. A Shay switching engine at the lower end of the incline grade moved loaded cars around to form a log train.

A railroad spur was built up the north side of the North Fork from the Portland Railway, Light & Power Company main line that connected to a trestle built across the North Fork River at the bottom of the incline.

In the spring of 1929, LaDee shipped at least thirty log cars a day to the Dwyer mill in southeast Portland, for a total of forty to forty-five thousand logs a day.

The loggers worked out of two camps. Camp no. 1 was located at the junction of the North Fork and the main stem Clackamas River, on the high ground six miles from Estacada. Camp no. 2 was located on a flat west of Winslow Creek, approximately six miles east of Camp no. 1. Logs from both camps were transported to the incline, where they were lowered down to the river.

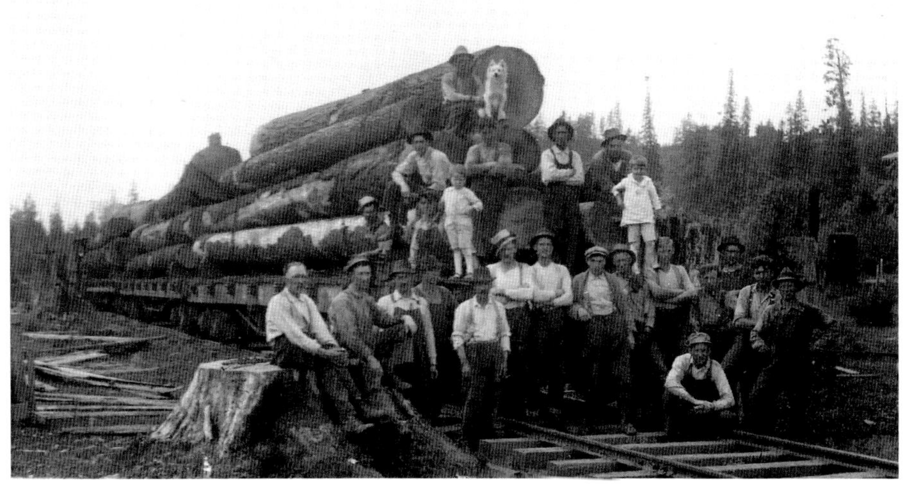

A rail car loaded with harvested old-growth timber awaits the train engine that will transport it to the mill. *Author's collection.*

It had been a dry summer. Mountains of slash and debris generated from the logging operation were left lying in the woods on LaDee Flat, cooked by the summer sun. In some places, the slash was ten feet deep, creating an enormous fire hazard. The condition concerned the U.S. Forest Service district ranger and his assistant, Thomas Carter, with good reason.

Wednesday, September 11, 1929, dawned clear and dry. Three hundred men were working in the woods that morning. About noon, a spark from the brake shoe on an engine started a fire one mile east of Camp no. 2, defying all efforts to check it. There was no loss of life, although there were several injuries. Clarence Vanderjack, a LaDee logging superintendent, was caught in the fire, and the hair was burned from his head. Continuing attempts to stop the flames were futile, and a fire blossomed.

Three hundred loggers quickly became firefighters. There were no airplanes to dip up huge buckets of water from the river or dump fire retardant to quell the flames. All the men had to work with were shovels, axes, picks, saws and courage.

Three yarding donkeys burned. A trestle on the logging railroad was completely burned, cutting off all rail traffic to Camp no. 2 and stranding the people living there. Loggers who lived in the camp were immediately engaged in the battle of their lives to keep the camp from being burned and the thirty-five people, including three women and two children, from being killed in the flames.

East winds pushed the fire toward Estacada and away from Camp no. 2. The fire took over a forest service work camp containing construction equipment for the first truck road being built in the Estacada Ranger District, along the ridge north of LaDee Flat.

The fire grew into an inferno that covered miles of railroad track and logging equipment on LaDee Flat. Logger Clarence Jubb related that the fire burned so hot in places that the rail curled like bacon. Flames wiped out all railroad trestles of LaDee logging and rendered all mountain trails inaccessible. Camp no. 1 was engulfed by flames. The only thing left was the bathhouse.

The fire raged and grew in size, leaping across the North Fork of the Clackamas River. Homeowners in the path of the flames did what they could to save their property. Frank Baker loaded his goods into his wagon and pushed it into the creek that ran by his house.

A road-building camp near the Bedford lookout tower was destroyed along with seven cars. The fire was completely out of control and had expanded from one thousand acres to three thousand acres.

On Thursday, September 12, the fire could be heard roaring in the North Fork canyon. Brands of fire flew overhead, and the wind was howling a gale. A fire headquarters was set up in the home of Carl Henrickson on Squaw Mountain Road near Garfield.

On Friday, three men trapped in a timbered section made their way to a stream and jumped into the water. They endured twenty-three hours with only their heads protruding from the surface. They survived, but their lungs were scorched. The fish did not fare so well. They floated on the surface, having been killed by the heat of the fire that raged along the stream.

On Saturday, flames could be seen leaping over the ridges to the south, and several spot fires were seen burning ahead of the main fire. The fire raged over Squaw Mountain, destroying a government camp and twenty autos belonging to firefighters.

The fire was consuming homes, barns, livestock and cabins. Household belongings, chickens in coops and as much as could be carried from the threatening flames were taken out by trucks. By midmorning, the fire became so thick and acrid that four hundred men east of Estacada were forced to retreat. The fire ran unchecked before the wind.

On Sunday, September 15, the dry east wind was blowing. In the southeast, a plume of smoke bellowed up into the sky, visible about ten miles away by Oliver Bowman at his home in Porter. The entire southeastern section of the sky was black with smoke. Oliver prepared to defend his home.

His family moved the stove and other heavy articles out of the house and into a clearing in the hopes that they would survive even if the house burned.

People living on the Clackamas abandoned their cabins and headed for Estacada, where flames from the fire were visible to the townspeople. Refugees soon numbered more than the city could accommodate. Estacada fire warden Mr. Armstrong appealed to Oregon City for assistance to fight the blaze. City manager J.L. Franzen gathered nineteen men, who were taken to the fire region.

By nightfall, the fire was within five miles of Estacada and closing in on the Garfield area. Some people buried belongings in an effort to save them. Rumors circulated that even some Estacada residents were preparing to move.

Firefighters, many bleeding from the nose, fought bravely on. Ray Van, fighting the fire with a government force of one hundred men, went insane battling the blaze and was taken to Oregon City by deputy sheriffs.

Mrs. W.W. Smith, chief operator Mrs. Alva Smith, Edith Marken and Lillian Harkenride, the four Estacada telephone operators, answered calls for assistance from people caught in the fire zone and gave information to concerned citizens on the status of the blaze. When not working on the switchboard, they assisted William Weingart, proprietor of the Estacada bake shop, in making sandwiches to be rushed to the fighting crews.

The fire, burning on two sides of Estacada, was sweeping westward. Pushed by the strong east wind, the fire exploded and swept through the forested hillsides, destroying close to fifteen thousand acres of timber. Log LaBarre Lodge was about a mile and a half above the old Garfield Grange. The lodge and the Tom Carter residence, both of them log structures, stood down the ridge in the path of the flames and were destroyed in spite of efforts to save them.

Mrs. Herbert Taylor, whose home was near Garfield on Squaw Mountain, phoned her son in St. Johns, pleading with him to come as quickly as possible. She and her husband, a crippled war veteran, worked desperately and tirelessly to defend the area around their property. Mr. Taylor fought until exhaustion overcame him. Not until his eyelashes, eyebrows and hair burned away did he give up the fight to save his house. Their son, who made a record drive to Garfield, was allowed to enter the fire zone. He was forced to drive through the flames and managed to get his parents, two brothers and one sister into the car just before the house erupted into flames. In order to make their escape, the family was forced to leave their chickens, four horses and the children's kittens.

Taylor returned to the veterans' hospital, where he had received medical treatment as a U.S. Navy veteran some time before. Flames swept over into Garfield. Six additional farms and homes succumbed to the flames, and the Garfield School fell victim to the fire.

The *Morning Enterprise* newspaper reported that, in addition to Log LaBarre and the Garfield School, numerous barns and garages were destroyed, as well as ten homes and farms, including those of Herbert Taylor, Benton Sarver, A.R. Rickeo, T. Whitney, A.W. Schunke, S.E. Reeher, M.C. Weatherby, J.W. Dillinger, Thomas Carter, Pat Flauty and J. McDonald.

During the day, it was feared that nearly two hundred men under the direction of T.H. Sherwood, supervisor of the Mount Hood Forest, were completely cut off.

The fire, covering more than twenty thousand acres, was now within three miles of Estacada.

On Monday, September 16, the Estacada fire headquarters sent a second call for help to Oregon City judge C.W. Kruse. Sheriff E.T. Nass moved road crews to aid in the effort. A spot of fire could be seen burning down Delph Creek in the vicinity of the trout hatchery, possibly a mile distant from the main fire.

More than nine hundred men now fought the inferno. Sixteen backfires were started to slow the spread of the fire, which was now only two miles from Estacada. To the relief of the men at fire headquarters, word reached them that Supervisor Sherwood and his men were safe.

Sometime in the early morning hours of Tuesday, September 17, the relentless wind died down, moist air drifted in and the fire was stopped before reaching Estacada. Fire had crept close to the Delph Creek trout hatchery, but it was saved as a result of the sudden change in wind. According to Judge Kruse, who surveyed a small portion of the fire-blackened area, "It is a deplorable sight. Farm houses are smoldering. Carcasses of livestock appear to have made vain efforts to escape from the flames."

By Wednesday, September 18, it was over. That morning, Estacada was considered safe and residents began to breathe easily for the first time in seven days. The telephone operators, who had stayed on the switchboard without sleep for as long as twenty-four hours, headed home to relax.

A relief crew of thirty-five firefighters headed out from the Zigzag Ranger Station with a string of pack mules loaded with supplies. The crew took over the mop-up job just north of the North Fork of the Clackamas River.

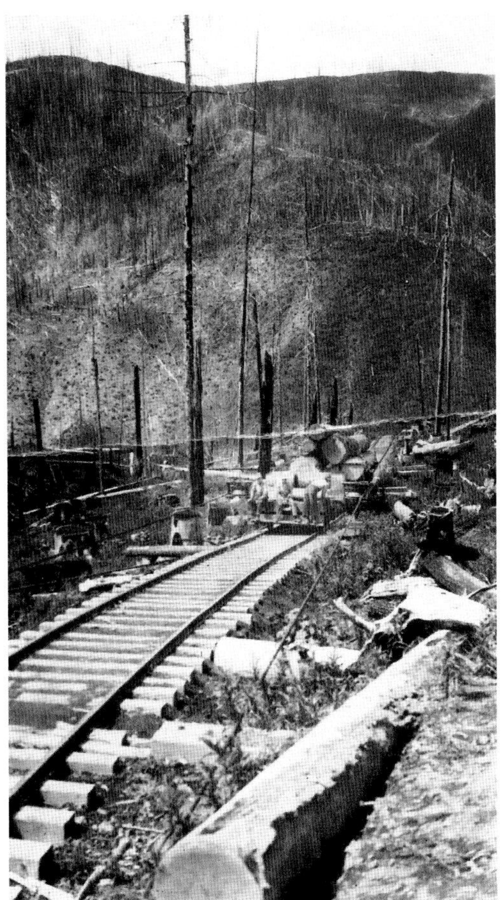

Left: Following the fire, men worked tirelessly to repair tracks and trestles so logs could be transported to the mills. *Courtesy of Jackknife-Zion-Horseheaven Historical Society.*

Below: Local Estacada residents drove up toward LaDee to view the devastation to the forest. *Courtesy of Jackknife-Zion-Horseheaven Historical Society.*

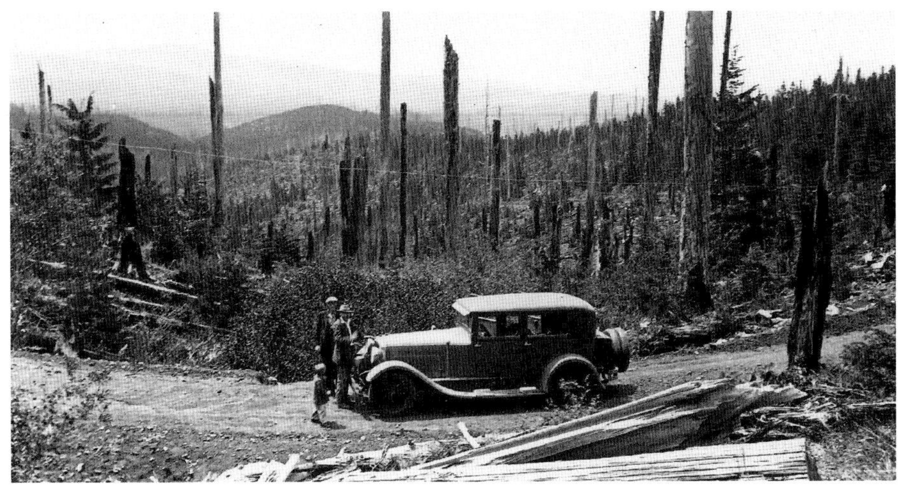

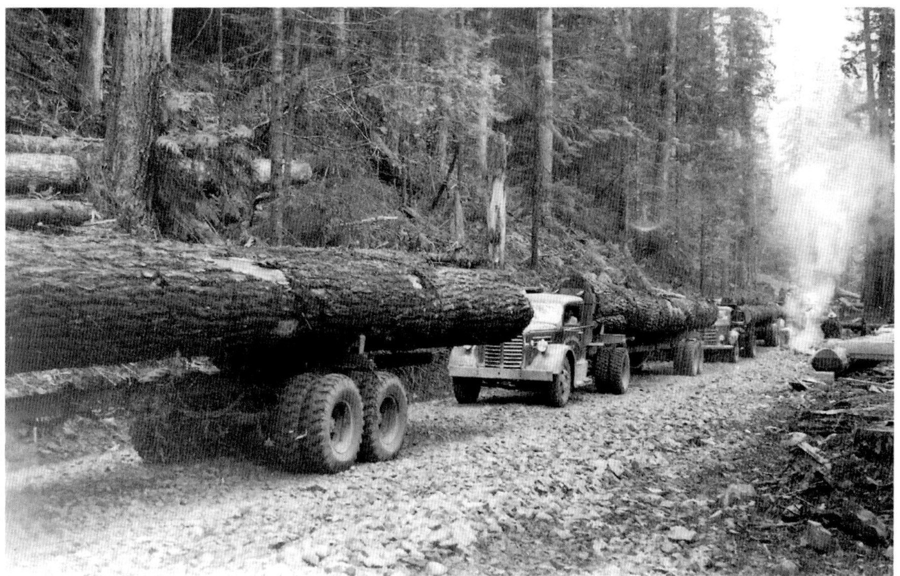

Within a month from the day the fire started, logging resumed and trucks rolled down the road to Estacada. *Author's collection.*

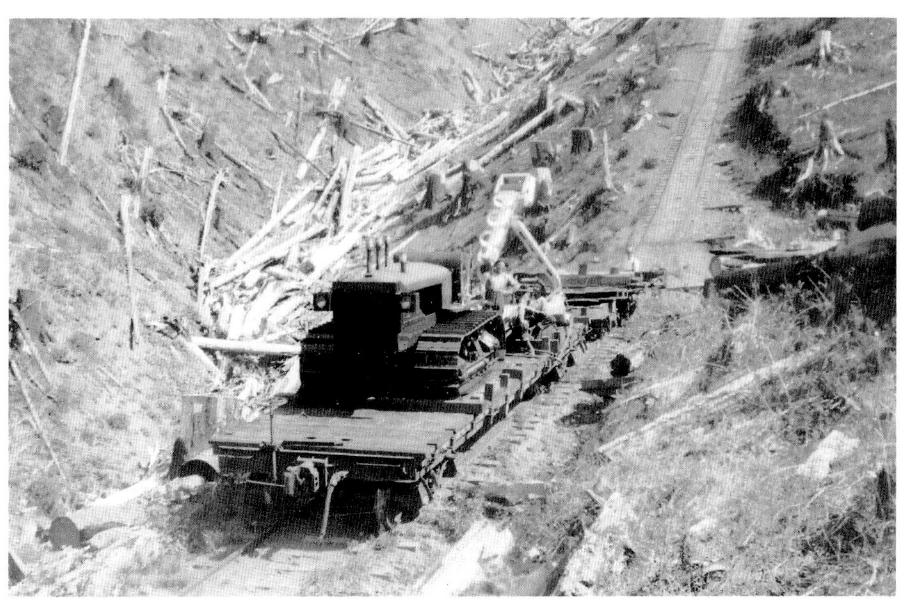

Ladee Logging Company operated this donkey engine on the long incline from the logging sites down to the Clackamas River. *Courtesy of Jack Reynolds.*

By the end of September, the fire had been reduced to a few smoldering stumps in a ten-mile-long, twenty-thousand-acre area. The total of forested land burned was estimated at between thirty and forty thousand acres.

As soon as the fire was brought under control and it was safe to enter the burned area, the loggers began the job of constructing new railroad trestles between Camp no. 2 and the incline. In little more than a month, LaDee had its logging operations working again and started shipping logs to the mills.

One logger paused from his work, surveyed the scorched, naked ground and grumbled, "Boy! Nearly forty thousand acres burned. We won't have fires like that up here anymore. It's a good thing—we'd soon be out of timber. Yeah, it's going fast."

Log LaBarre

Log LaBarre Hotel. The very mention of the name evokes an image of elegance and entertainment. Even after the passage of one hundred years, Estacada residents still talk about its existence.

Harry A. LaBarre was an entrepreneur who loved the good life and dreamed of a resort that would attract visitors to the 120-acre parcel of land that he and his wife, Minnie, owned. The property was located just six miles from Estacada, at an elevation of fourteen hundred feet up Squaw Mountain.

Harry contracted with Minnie's nephew Thomas "Tom" Carter, a forester and engineer, to build an imposing structure filled with amenities. Calling on his knowledge and expertise, Tom created a three-story lodge measuring sixty feet wide by seventy feet in length, made of mammoth logs, with ceilings of heavy beams. The windows of thirty-five cozy rooms looked out on porches that ran the entire length and sides of the building. Baths had hot and cold running water. A small grocery store conveniently stood nearby. Construction cost a total of $12,000. Next door to the hotel, Tom built a log home as his own residence.

The hotel opened in June 1915. LaBarre advertised it as a fishing and hunting resort. Guests arriving from Portland on the electric line would be met on request by the LaBarre automobile, which would transport them through the beautiful scenery in upper Garfield. Hotel postcards described it as a "delightful place to spend summer or winter."

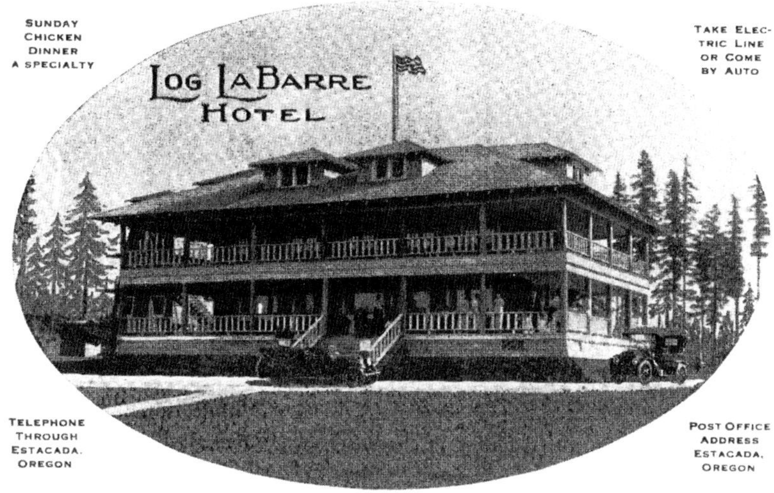

This postcard shows the luxurious Log LaBarre resort hotel, which drew vacationers and weekend tourists from the Portland area and beyond. *Courtesy of Sylvia Bowman.*

Visitors who wanted to venture out from Estacada could drive to the resort, where, the postcards declared, "Sunday Dinner is a Specialty." The cook intimated that, for male guests, the hotel also offered a different kind of female specialty, available every day of the week. Sadly, Log LaBarre was one of the victims of the August 1929 fire that swept across the area from LaDee flats. Harry and Minnie were not at home that day. Tom Carter, assistant supervisor of the Mount Hood National Forest at the time, alerted the hotel's employees and guests, who could only flee down Squaw Mountain as the flames burned Harry's grand hotel to the ground.

TRIBUTE

Schools of the late 1800s and early 1900s were more than just buildings. They were more than places where students learned reading, arithmetic, geography, writing, history and deportment. Community programs, events and social gatherings were often held at the local school. Losing one could be devastating, and such was the case for Garfield in September 1929.

Students had resumed their yearly classes. Days were still warm enough to play games outside during recess. The warm days also could cause a body to feel drowsy while trying to concentrate during the afternoon lesson.

On the morning of Thursday, September 18, all pupils were fully awake. News was circulating through Garfield that a fire had started the day before at LaDee Flats. Word spread as quickly as the flames, becoming more dire with each passing day. On Friday, it was reported that the conflagration was moving down Squaw Mountain. On Saturday, some residents in Estacada were considering leaving. And on Sunday, the fire was a mile and a half above Garfield.

Early Monday morning, catastrophe struck. There would be no school that day.

The flames that had been licking their way down the mountain, devouring farm after farm, arrived at the Garfield School. Don Eaden, who participated in the effort to save the building, described what happened. An ember flew from the trees uphill and lit on the roof. Soon, a tongue of flame rose toward the sky. There was no ladder tall enough for anyone to climb up to the roof, so no one could reach the fire to put it out. Neighbors could only stand by helplessly as their precious school collapsed into ashes. Inexplicably, the covered play structure remained standing.

It was a pitiful sight. The only things remaining were two chimneys and a smoldering ruin. During the coming days, everyone stared in disbelief at the blackened earth where the school had stood. Students and teacher began sharing stories about their experiences there. Some felt there should be a permanent way of remembering.

Eventually, they joined to create a tribute. Someone produced a metal box about twelve inches square into which the students and teacher placed their memorials. Included were things retrieved from the burnt wreckage: a parched picture of George Washington; a partial scrap of cursive writing that once graced the border above the blackboard; the remnant of a pencil. Others brought items in remembrance of the year 1929. One girl contributed a beautiful new hair ribbon. A boy gave a ball he and his chums would have played with in the schoolyard. A teacher brought the front page of the *Morning Enterprise* newspaper that described the fire. One by one, the children and their teacher placed their keepsakes in the box.

They buried the box in front of the bare ground where the school had stood and planted a young tree nearby as a living memorial.

After the 1929 fire, Don and Helen Eaden bought the Garfied property and built a home on the site of the former school. Don framed the play structure into a shed.

The Eadens lived there until they sold their property in the 1990s. As she prepared to leave, Helen pointed out a venerable bigleaf maple tree near Divers Road and advised the new owner, "If that tree ever falls down, look for the box."

A Couple of Joes

It happened only when his wife, Nettie, left the room. Winking at his grandchildren and whispering "Shhh," Joe pulled off his hollow wooden leg, retrieved the pint of whiskey nestled inside, threw back a slug, returned the bottle to its hiding place and strapped the leg back on.

Joseph "Joe" Rickey Sr. had worked for the U.S. Forest Service. His primary assignment was building fire watchtowers on the wild mountaintops in the Mount Hood National Forest. One year, after his tower was completed, he hand-carved eight bathing tubs at Bagby Hot Springs out of large cedar logs he had felled.

Every summer, a twenty-mule team would cart Rickey, lumber and supplies deep into the woods and leave him there to do his job. At the end of the summer, the mule team went back to cart him out, along with barrels of cured meat and fish he had hunted, fished and prepared for his family's winter food.

Joe lost his leg in a horrific accident in the early 1940s. It happened in the forest service motor pool shop. As he walked to the tool bench in front of the truck he was working on, the truck jumped out of gear, lurched off its block and pinned Joe against the bench. Despite the excruciating pain, he was able to grab some metal bars off the bench and, using his own strength, slowly lever the truck away from his body. He thought he must have passed out several times, but he was able to crawl to a primitive phone and call for help. His leg was crushed. The doctors did what they could, but eventually it developed gangrene, and they were forced to remove it. Fortunately, they were able to fit him with a wooden leg.

His disability did not stop him. Since he could no longer work in logging, he began going "downtown" every day, to do odd jobs. He hung out with his friends in the manner of all small-town residents, sitting on

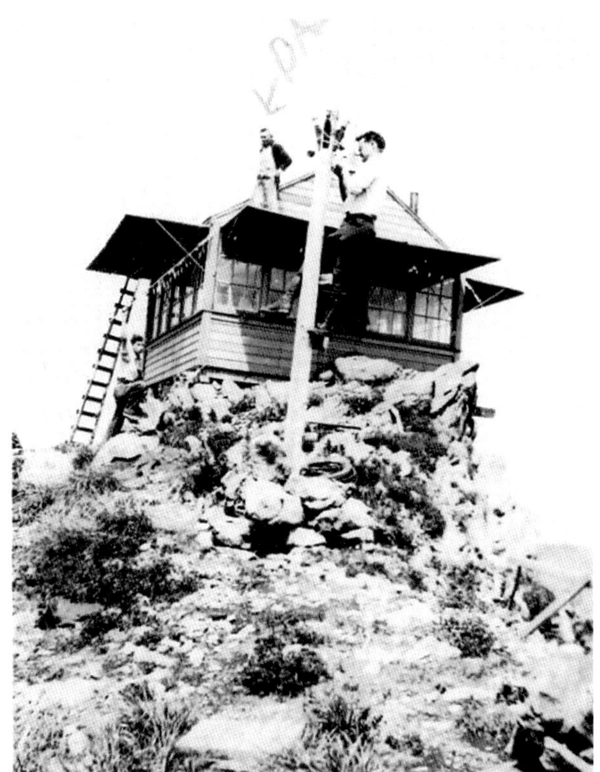

Left: This lookout tower is one of many that Joseph Rickey built on the mountaintops for the U.S. Forest Service. *Courtesy of Alice Neely*.

Below: Joe Rickey sometimes hung out at the barbershop with Alva Smith, co-owner of Cascade Telephone & Telegraph across the street. *Courtesy of Alice Neely*.

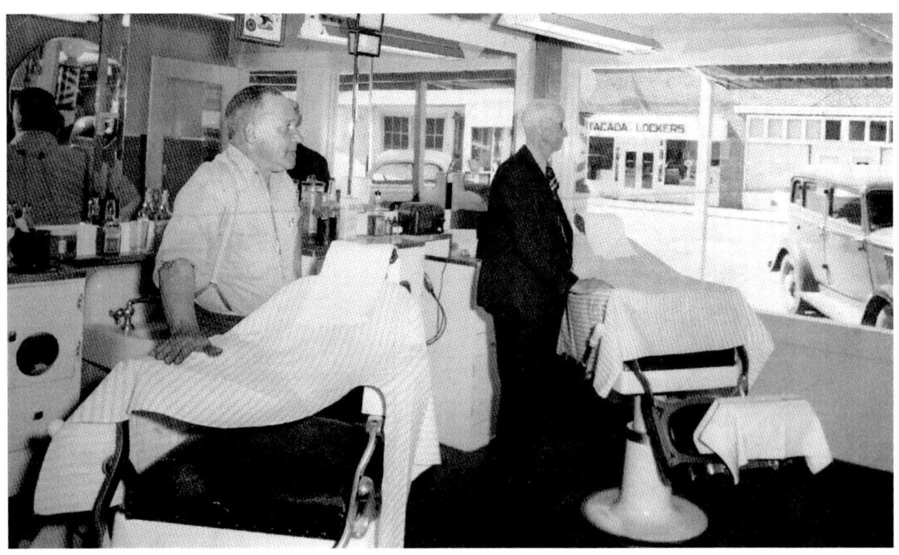

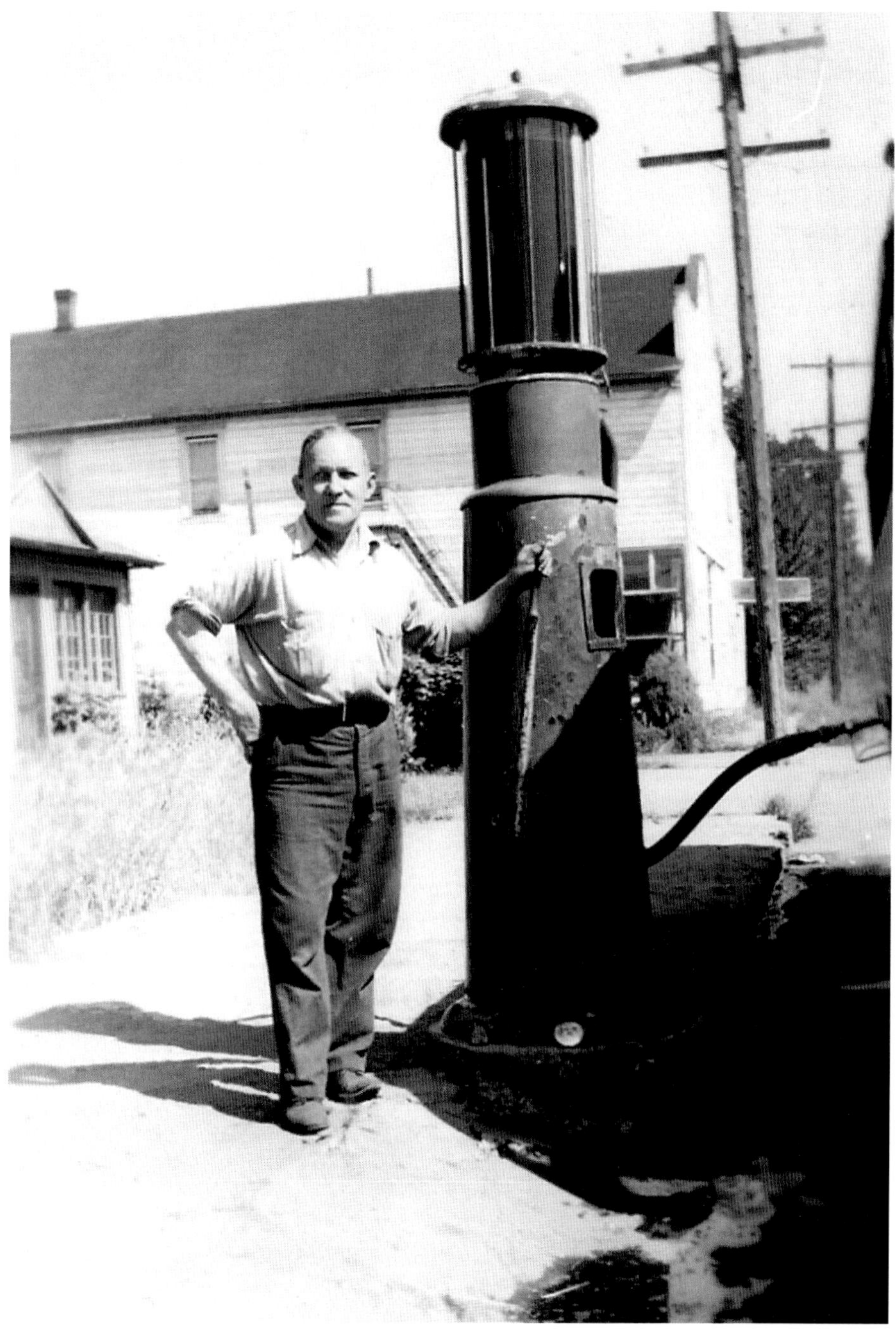

In addition to operating his newsstand at the bus station, Joseph Rickey pumped gas for the buses. *Courtesy of Alice Neely.*

a bench in front of the bus depot, "Mayberry style." The barbershop, across the street from Estacada Lockers and the telephone company, often served as a place to jaw with friends. Over the years, Joe became a much-loved downtown fixture.

Even with cordial companions, sitting around was hard on a man who had always been on the move, building tangible things. An enterprising, energetic fellow, he soon started a small newsstand at the bus station, selling papers, magazines and cigarettes. He also pumped gas for the buses. He reported that this pursuit was more fun than staying at home, especially with a Methodist teetotaler wife.

Joe met his wife, Nettie Bell Woodle, in Portland in 1919 while she was training to be a legal secretary. Nettie was the granddaughter of the Howletts and the Woodles, both Oregon Trail pioneers. According to Currinsville residents, the families were "snobs." Nettie's parents, Joseph Palmer Woodle and Lydia Howlett, were not amused when their daughter fell for an ordinary Joe. They were dismayed when she actually married the man. Apparently, they were also not impressed that, after the Civil War, one of Joe's relatives had invented a well-known drink called a "Gin Rickey."

Nettie Bell, an intelligent woman, worked as a highly respected court clerk to the judge in Estacada following Joe's forestry accident. At home, tendrils of lovely sweet peas climbed the back fence surrounding her prolific vegetable beds, and no cook could match her fried rabbit. Although she

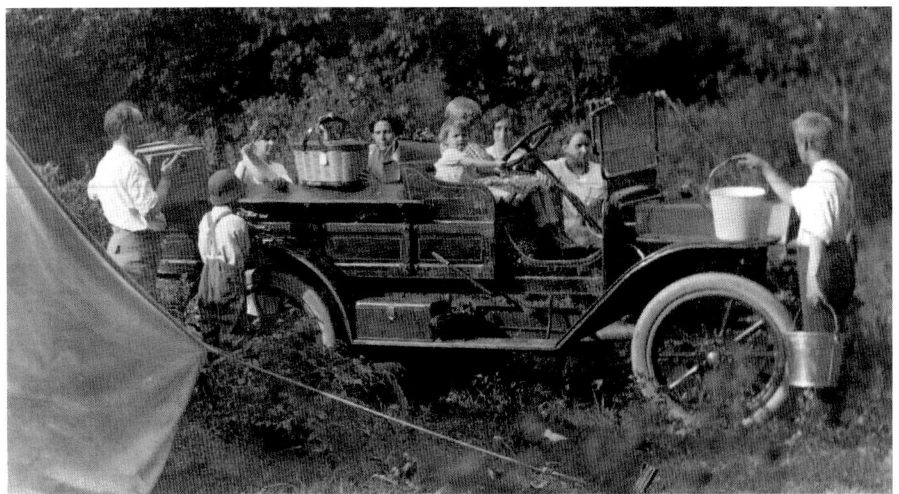

Nettie Bell Woodle with her family at a campout in the woods above Estacada in 1918. *Courtesy of Alice Neely.*

grew much of the family's food, she was extremely frugal, carefully allotting one-half a potato and one pork chop per person.

When not at work at Estacada City Hall or tending her garden, she was on the couch, reading voraciously. In the 1950s and '60s, when her grandchildren spent summers there, she introduced them to liverwurst sandwiches and the Estacada library. The kids earned twenty-five cents for doing chores, which they spent on banana splits at the soda fountain inside the pharmacy, then went to read at the library.

After Joe and Nettie wed, they settled in her hometown of Estacada. Together, they raised five sons, all of whom became World War II heroes. The youngest of the boys, a "love child," was named Joseph Carr Rickey after his father, Joe Sr.

At age ten, Joe Jr. worked in the woods as the lumberjacks' "Whistle Punk," operating the signal wire running to the donkey engine whistle. Every summer, beginning at age twelve, he worked on an eastern Oregon ranch

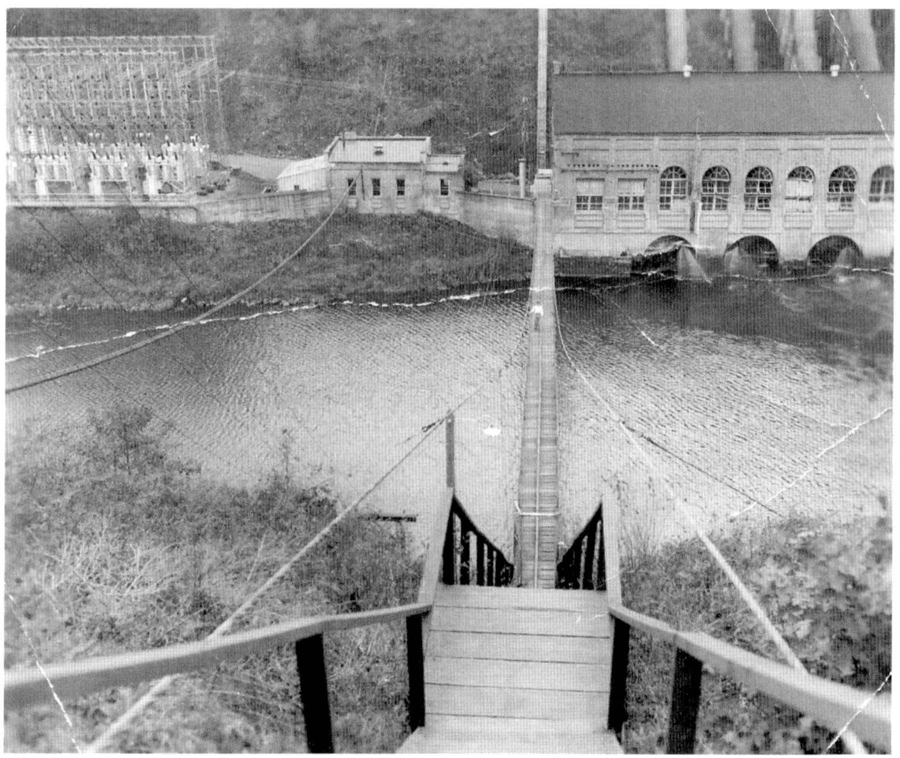

A swinging footbridge across the Clackamas River allowed workers to cross from their houses to the Faraday Dam. *Courtesy of Alice Neely.*

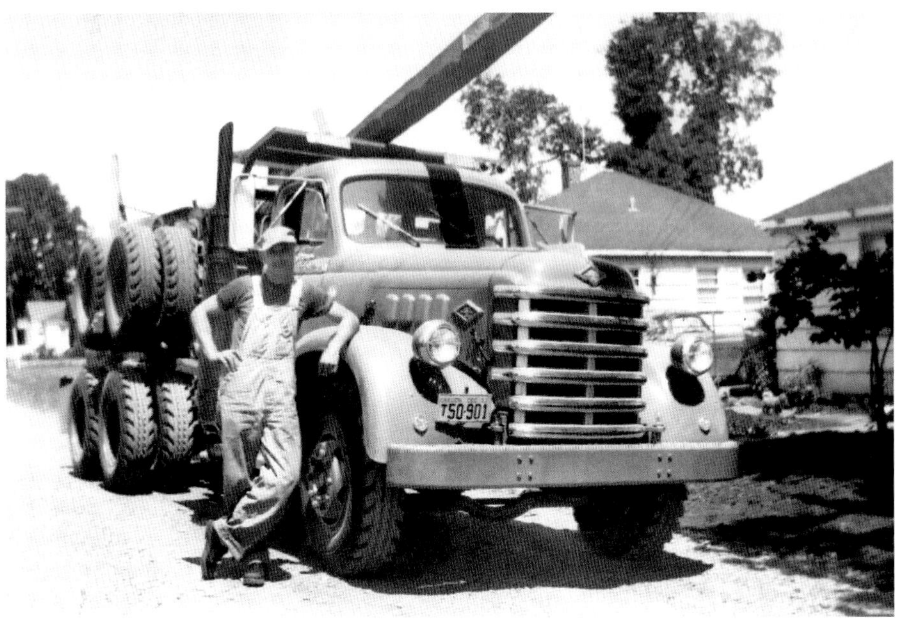

Proud Joe Rickey Jr. made sure he had a photo of his new truck as he started his own logging business. *Courtesy of Alice Neely.*

to help support his family—and buy clothes! He stopped by his homosexual uncle's in Portland on his way home to get advice on the latest fashions.

He was a charmer, a tennis player, a clarinet man and outgoing "Fred Astaire" of Estacada. As if he were not popular enough, Joe Jr. had multiple copies of his senior high school photo made. He tied them with bows and handed them out to all the girls, telling each they were the only one. Everyone adored him until his death at the age of ninety-four, when he was still flirting with his hospice nurses.

After Joe Jr. came home from the war, he returned to Estacada, where he married his childhood sweetheart, Lois Nash. Like many local men, Joe went to work as an operator for Portland General Electric. The couple lived in the company housing at the dam, next door to the boss, Russell Reed.

However, after a time, Joe Jr. tired of his job at the dam, so he began driving a logging truck, eventually investing in his own rig. Like his father before him, he was drawn to the forest, which is where he spent his life.

Like most of us, neither father nor son gained fame for anything they did. But they sired children who carried with them the Rickey attributes of strength, fortitude, patriotism, sense of adventure, optimism and love of family. Not too bad for a couple of Joes.

Bus Depot

Abraham "Abe" Ames owned the Broadway Service Garage, where mechanics filled automobiles with gasoline, air and water and handled vehicle repairs. Abe owned the garage but spent most of his time in his plumbing and metal workshop next door. Across the front of the garage was a sign: "Portland Estacada Truck Terminal." A smaller Greyhound-type bus entered the building from the rear and exited onto the street in front. A hardware store was to the left, and up the street on the corner was the small house that held the Estacada Library. Abe Ames was town constable at the time River Mill was under construction. He spoke of how rough the town was back then. He served as mayor of Estacada for one or more terms beginning in 1947.

Lookout

"On a clear day, you can see the whole Cascade Range from up here" said Denise Wilson in an August 1980 interview for the *Oregonian*. Anyone who had been a fire spotter in the Mount Hood National Forest would probably echo her comment.

Use of the fire towers began in the early 1900s. A spotter high on a mountaintop had an excellent view of smoke or fire within the Mount Hood forest. By the 1930s, more than one hundred lookouts spent countless hours watching for wildfires.

Spotters and all their supplies were carried in on horseback or on foot. Accommodations were rustic, and at elevations as high as 5,500 feet, nights were very cold even on the hottest days. There was no water on a mountaintop, so spotters had to hike or ride to a lower elevation to refill their water containers from a stream or lake.

The worst part, if one could call it that, was being completely alone for months. Occasional visits from forest rangers or friends who brought steaks and cold beer relieved what little boredom a spotter may have felt.

The scenery was magnificent and the air invigorating. Those who spent a summer as a lookout treasured the peaceful seclusion and returned year after year.

For years, the Clackamas River Ranger District relied on lookouts in fire towers to spot smoke or fire and alert the rangers, but aerial observation gradually replaced land-based spotters. By 2016, the only actively manned tower remaining in the Clackamas River Ranger District was at Sisi Butte.

Aerial observation is "progress," but former volunteers say they miss spending three glorious months looking out over the forests and feeling nothing but tranquility.

Jigs Pederson served as a U.S. Forest ranger for decades. In 1976, when the forest service brought out a new replacement manual, Jigs was not impressed. He was quoted as saying, "In my day, the manual was just a little book. That was back when a man had to use his head to do things."

PACKING

Men who earned their livelihood as packers were a breed apart. They lived in solitude, spending weeks or even months in the forest with only their horses or mules as company.

Jack Akins was a U.S. Forest Service packer, but he did not use horses. For over thirty years, he and his string of mules carried supplies, including

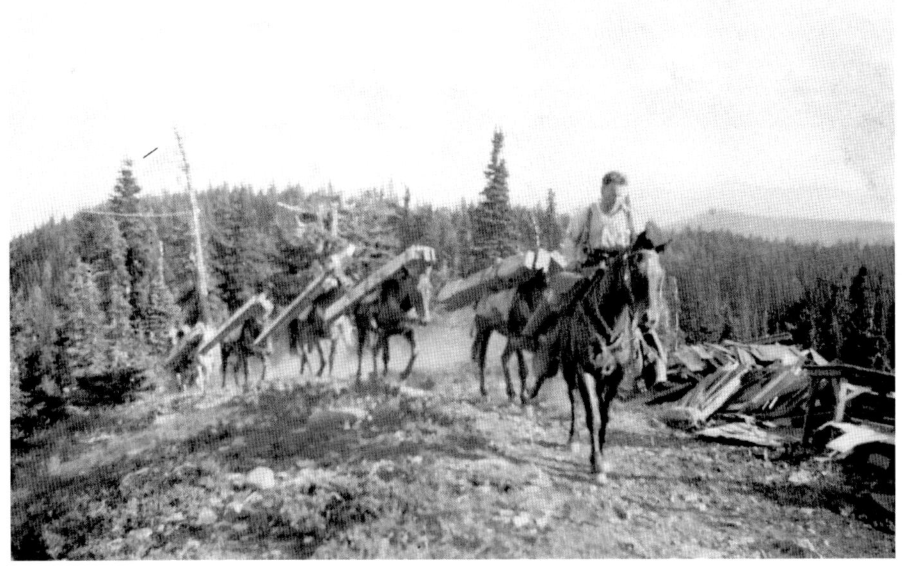

Jack Akins single-handedly loaded his string of pack mules with twelve-foot-long four-by-six timbers to deliver to the Mount Hood District U.S. Forest Service. *Courtesy of Bob Akins.*

twelve-foot lengths of four- by six-inch lumber, to trail crews and lookout stations in the Mount Hood Ranger District. Timbers had to be perfectly balanced and stable, for once the animals moved, the load could shift and be lost, or the mules might be injured.

Jack was such an expert packer that in 1951, he loaded a mule with a cooking stove and went all the way to Ollalie Lake. Everyone survived the journey, and the crew at the lake was happy to have a stove.

FEELING ALIVE

"It's hard, it's dangerous, and it's a challenge that makes a man feel alive." That is why a man becomes a logger, according to Chet French, who shared his thoughts in a 1984 interview for *Clackamas County News*.

A logger rises at three in the morning and does not see his bed again until after eight at night. At the logging area, he sees the spar tree, a 160-foot-tall tree stripped of all branches, or one of the metal spar poles that began replacing the spar tree in 1980. The pole is the highest anchor point in a high-lead logging setup and supports the lead blocks with its cables rigged to haul logs up the hill. It is steadied by guy wires and resembles a circus tent awaiting its cover.

One man operates the donkey engine winch, bringing bundles of logs up the hill from where they were cut. A whistle-punk on the donkey engine toots out distinctive signals that announce logs coming uphill, a log swung into position or a log deposited. Another man operates a giant claw loader and stacks the logs, sorting them by diameter into decks, or piles, according to the mill's requirements. He loads the logs by claw onto the trucks waiting to transport them to the lumber mills.

Out in the forest are the men, like Chet, who cut the trees down. Before they start the job, the mill's timber buyer goes over the timber sale and tells the men the lengths the mill wants from the standing trees. Good cutters can look at a living tree and picture it in board fee. Chet said, "We size up the tree, checking the path of its fall, and then make our cuts. Two cuts—a ninety degree and a forty-five degree—make the face. This wedge is knocked out. Another cut from the back sends the tree over."

Yelling "Timber!" as a warning to any other men in the area, the cutters watch warily as the trees, some as tall as 160 feet, fall toward the earth. A Douglas fir is heavy and falls so hard that the newly cut butt tip

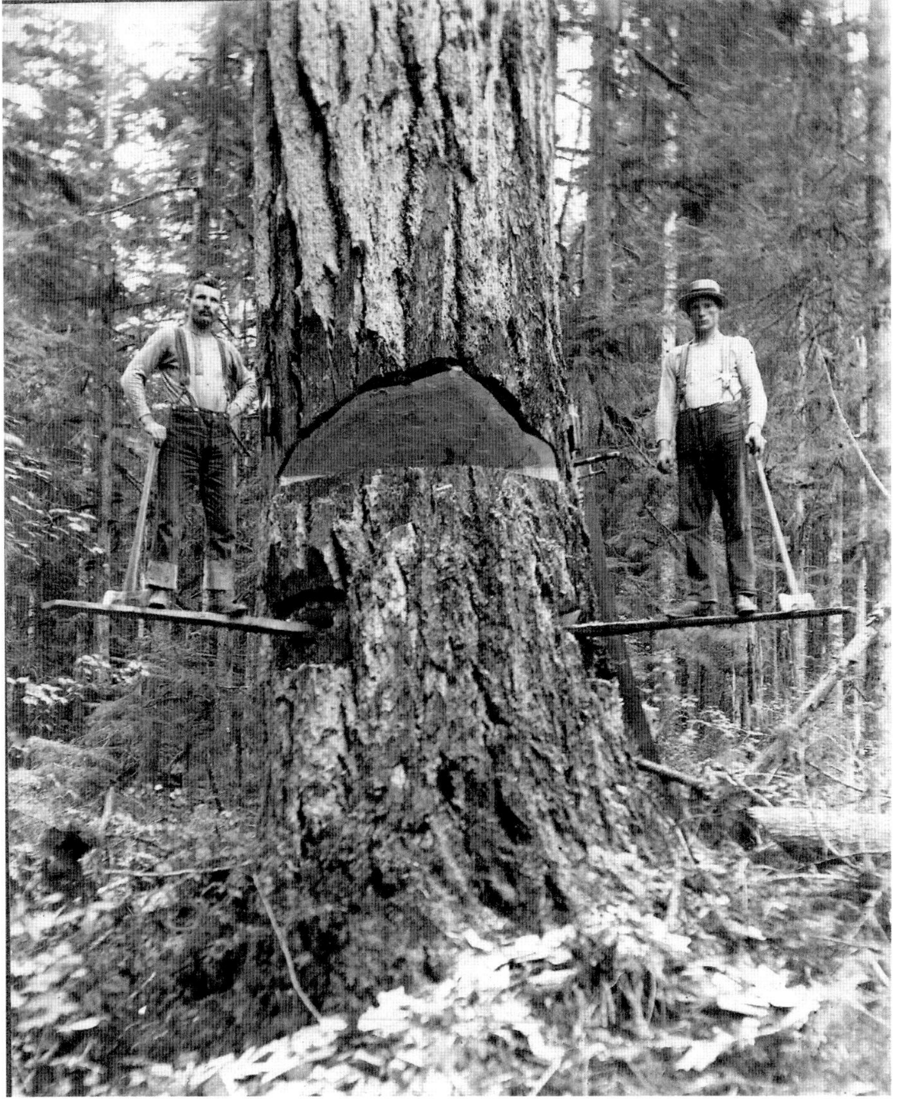

In the 1800s, fallers cut notches in old-growth trees to hold springboards, on which men stood while sawing. *Courtesy of Jackknife-Zion-Horseheaven Historical Society.*

will dangerously bounce back up quite a few feet before settling on the forest floor.

The best cutter has an active mind, imagination and a desire to do the work right so no one gets hurt. But men do get hurt, caught by a falling tree, injured by a bucking saw or falling from what seemed to be safe footing.

These men risk their lives and are often scared to death. They are working with awesome power, not only with the trees, but the tools they use, and they are, after all, puny humans. Loggers have a saying: When you are hurt in the woods, you are hurt for a long time.

"It's hard, it's dangerous and it's a challenge that makes a man feel alive." That is why a man becomes a logger.

Timber

For eight decades, logging was the main industry in Estacada. The high point was in the 1950s. In 1955, the acreage in the Mount Hood National Forest totaled 1,183,886. Standing timber equaled 25 billion board feet. The actual timber cut was 189 million board feet. Logging companies used sky-line yarding, donkey yarding and cat yarding to pull out the downed trees.

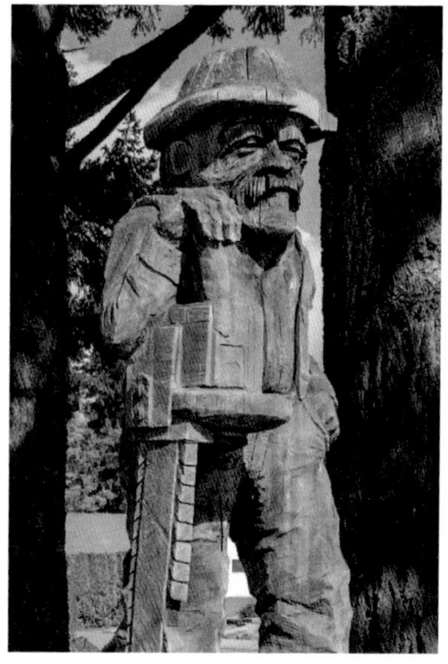

An eight-foot-tall carving by Bobby Lehnen in front of Estacada City Hall is a tribute to Estacada's timber heyday. *Courtesy of Mike Dille.*

Twenty-five major logging operations, including Acme Timber, Glen Park, Silver Tip, Guy Keller, Dwyer and Tony Fernandez, took advantage of the abundant timber.

During the summer months, as many as two hundred trucks, with each truck load averaging 5,000 board feet, passed through Estacada every day on their way to the mills, delivering between 750,000 and 1 million board feet of lumber.

Logging and everything associated with it continues to be part of Estacada's identity. Many people experienced it, and many more residents still tell the stories about the eighty years of glory, when timber was king in Estacada.

Raven

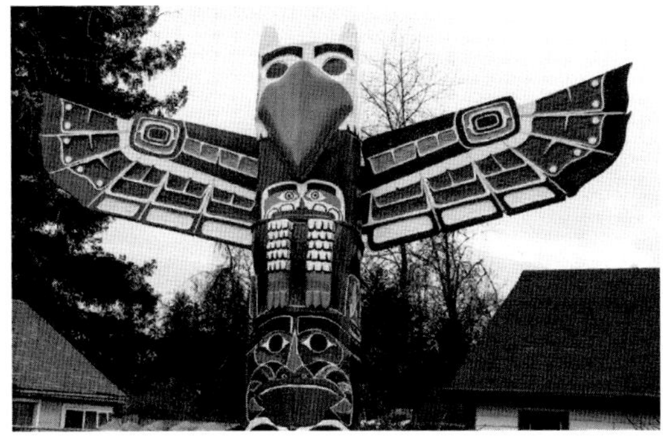

This totem pole, carved by Jonathan Birchfield, stands on the north side of Highway 224 in Estacada. *Courtesy of Mike Dille.*

It seems strange. No one in town remembers Bob Raven Peaseley. He was director of the Indian Arts Studies Center in Estacada and lived here prior to a fire that destroyed his studio and home in 1979. He was a Native American master carver who earned the title after intensive study.

In 1964, at the age of thirty-two, he retired from the Battleground, Washington police department to begin his journey. He served five years as an apprentice to four master carvers, including Chief Don Lalooska Smith and Duane Pasco. He lived in tribal villages on Washington's west coast, in British Columbia and in Sitka, Alaska, absorbing the subtleties of their carving arts.

His ceremonial masks and carvings, such as *Raven* and *Fog Woman*, were acclaimed throughout the country, sweeping three national competitions for carvers sponsored by Inter-Tribal Ceremonial in Gallup, New Mexico, in 1976. Bob Peaseley's mastery of the carvings of the seven tribes ranked him among the master carvers in America. He was a lecturer in coastal Indian art and legends at Colorado State University in 1977 and 1978.

In 1979, a fire destroyed his home and studio, and with them the ceremonial masks and ceremonial costumes he had made, the button blankets, tools, collections of manuscripts, and photos and slides of his work.

It seems strange. No one in town remembers Bob Raven Peaseley.

Bibliography

Adams, B. "Estacada's New Library: The Heart of the Community." *OLA Quarterly* 13, no. 3 (2014): 20–21.

Carr, William F. "Logging for the Union: A History of the Porter-Carstens and LaDee Logging Companies." *OLA Quarterly* (January 1991). USDA Forest Service, Pacific Northwest Region, Mount Hood National Forest.

Page, Adrianne. "Of Owl Chiefs, and Wind Gods, and Cedar and Bone." *Northwest*, August 15, 1982.

Paulin, Pamela K. "Boring to the Core; the Archeology, History, and Dendrochronology of a Railroad Logging Camp, LaDee Flat, Clackamas County." An abstract of the thesis for the degree of master of arts in Interdisciplinary Studies in Anthropology and Geography presented on June 7, 2007. Oregon State University.

Scrivener, Kate. "Logging." *Clackamas County News*, July 18, 1984.

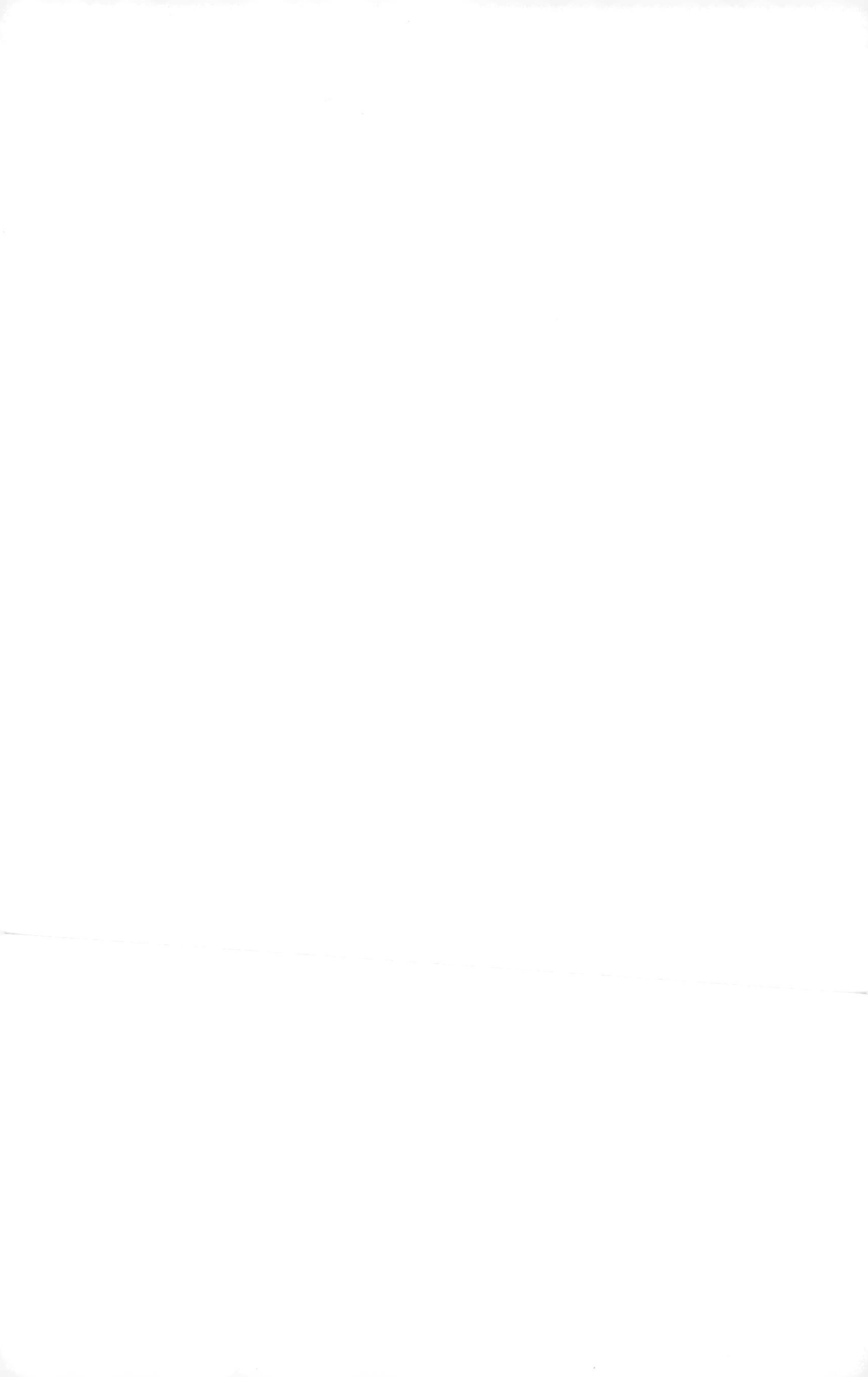

Index

About the Author

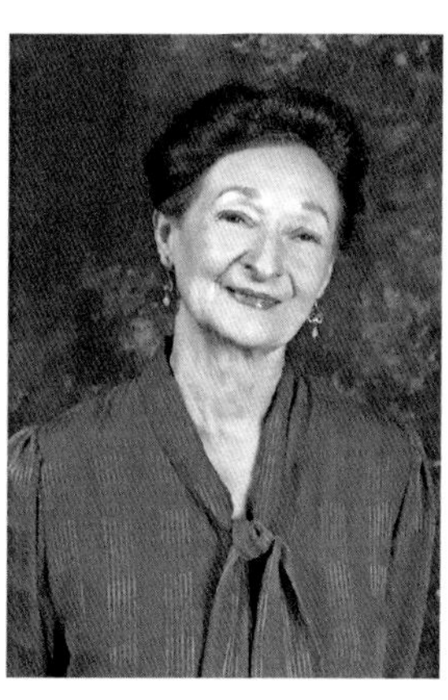

Kathryn Hurd thrives on research, personal interviews, variety and the challenge of telling a good story. She has four other books to her credit, as well as stories for newspapers.

Briarwood: A Neighborhood Remembered (1998) details the evolution of an area over a one-hundred-year span, based on interviews conducted with current and past residents. In *Bruno Paul John: An Oregon Legacy* (2000), she traced the life of B.P. John, who was instrumental in bringing Portland, Oregon, into prominence in the national furniture manufacturing industry. Anthony J. Dwyer was a pioneer in the logging and sawmilling industry. *The Dwyers: Pioneers in the Timber Industry* (2004) is his story. Through the family's private collections of personal papers, photos and news accounts, the account of the Dwyer era was brought to life. *Images of America: Estacada* (2012) was the first professionally produced book on the history of Estacada. Previously unpublished photographs and historical captions presented a 150-year overview of the city and its surrounding area.

Kathryn's articles in print include, among others, "Squaw Mountain Road Culvert Replaced" in *Clackamas County News*; "Artist in the Gravel" in *Sand & Gravel* magazine; and "The Box We Couldn't Wait to Open" in the *Christian Science Monitor*.

She was a professional storyteller for over fifty years. Kathryn rewrote popular Russian fairy tales, which she recorded in a compilation titled *Stories from the Hearth*. The recording was awarded the 1995 Parents Choice Gold Award.

Kathryn Hurd is a member of the Willamette Writers and the Society of Children's Book Writers and Illustrators. Her current project is collecting accounts of the Estacada area with the goal of creating historical books for children and adults.

She writes at her home on twenty acres in rural Clackamas County, which she shares with three dogs, two cats, two parrots, two horses, laying hens and abundant wildlife.